THE WORDS AND WONDERS OF THE CROSS

by GORDON H. GIROD

BAKER BOOK HOUSE
Grand Rapids, Michigan

PHOTOLITHOPRINTED BY CUSHING - MALLOY, INC.
ANN ARBOR, MICHIGAN, UNITED STATES OF AMERICA
1 9 7 9

To the five people whom I have neglected
in order that this book might be written,
my wife and our four children,
Stephen, Lynne Ellen, Gerald and Carol,
this book is dedicated with my love.

Preface

By one method of accounting "seven words" were spoken at Calvary. These are the familiar "seven words" spoken by our Lord from the cross beginning with, "Father, forgive them..." and concluding with, "Into thy hands I commend my Spirit." Though largely neglected as such, five additional words were spoken at the cross. Even as the Son spoke seven times from the cross, so the Father spoke five times from above.

"He spake, and it was done," declares the Word of God. Indeed, and thus God spake at Calvary. He spake, and the earth was cast into darkness at midday. He spake again, and the veil of the temple was inexplicably rent in twain. He spake, and the earth did quake, and the rocks were rent. He spake, and the graves were opened. After the resurrection of our Lord (which one might call the mightiest word), God spake once more, and many bodies of the saints were raised.

Thus one might speak of the "twelve words" at Calvary, seven spoken by the Son while He made atonement for human sin, and five spoken by the Father while "God was in Christ reconciling the world unto Himself."

These two, the words of our Lord and the supernatural events which transpired about the cross, are of course closely related. Our Lord's words speak to the heart of his redemptive work. Their effect is reinforced by the mighty works God wrought even as the Beloved Son affixed the handwriting of our sins to the cross in his own blessed body. Taken together, "The Words and Wonders of the Cross" complement and supplement each other to provide a comprehensive overview of "Jesus Christ and Him crucified."

Gordon H. Girod

Contents

1. Father,
Forgive My Sheep

Father, forgive them; for they know not what they do.
—Luke 23:34

The "seven sayings" of Jesus from the cross, sometimes called the "seven last words," form the basis for some of the most universal preaching in Christendom. The "words" of Christ are expounded annually from a multitude of pulpits. Each "Good Friday" services are conducted in churches throughout the nation. In such services, almost without exception, the Scriptural basis of the preaching is the "seven words" of Christ from the cross. At least once each year, therefore, we can be certain that almost everyone will have opportunity to hear these texts expounded.

Unfortunately, much bad preaching is done on these texts. Perhaps this is accounted for, at least in part, because the preacher attempts to present "new material" or at least a fresh approach" to the subject. Sometimes the desire for novelty may supersede the boundaries prescribed by careful interpretation. More basic to the problem, however, is the fact that these are difficult texts to treat. Admittedly, the undiscerning expositor will encounter no difficulty in dealing with them. He merely treats them superficially, developing them in topical fashion, the topic often bearing little intrinsic relationship to the truth revealed in them. Again, some go astray, because they treat the "seven words" as isolated statements rather than taking the full Biblical context into consideration. If, however, one would do full justice to the "words" of Christ, if he would plumb their depths and bring forth their treasure,

11

he will find himself confronted with a task which is both difficult and rewarding.

The errors which occur in treating the first "word" from the cross may be grouped in two categories. The first are those which misinterpret the prayer of Jesus, "Father, forgive them, for they know not what they do." The second and closely related misconception centers about the identity of those for whom Christ offered this prayer. Before we undertake to deal with the "problem" areas of the first word from the cross, we shall pay heed to two introductory considerations.

Consider first the unusual character of the words of Christ as expressions from the lips of a dying man. Perhaps this can best be seen by comparison and contrast. During the past decade capital punishment has been raised as an issue by editors and feature writers. Among the multiplicity of articles which have appeared in the popular press was one which presented short biographical portraits of men who were about to die for their crimes against society. These were dramatic accounts of the tensions, the hopes and fears that haunt men who are about to die.

More significant for our purpose are the "last words" these men spoke as they were about to die. A few said nothing. They had pled their case. Their plea had been denied. They faced death as they had faced life — hard, cold, almost devoid of human sensitivity. Others reacted emotionally. At the last moment one cried, "I am innocent. I swear before God I am innocent!" Then his cries subsided into muffled sobs. Some became weak and limp, so that they had to be assisted into the execution chamber. One took the long walk down "death row" as his last opportunity for escape. He struggled and fought each step of the way. From the electric chair itself he snarled, "I'll see you all in hell."

Reactions such as these we can understand. We may not approve of them, but we can understand them as human reactions to death by execution. How different, then, were the words of Christ: "Father, forgive them, for they know not what they do. . . . Today thou shalt be with me in paradise. . . . Woman, behold thy son. Son, behold thy mother. . . .

My God, my God why hast thou forsaken me?...I thirst....
It is finished.... Into thy hands I commend my spirit...."

These certainly rank among the most unusual words ever
to be spoken by a man who was about to die. Indeed, the
adjectives "strange" and "unusual" do not adequately describe
the words of Christ from the cross. One should recognize a
uniqueness in these "words." Even in Scripture one finds
nothing quite like them with the exception of the words of
Stephen who was the first of the martyrs to follow his
Lord in death, and who evinced a similar spirit toward his
persecutors.

In the main the Scriptures are silent concerning the death
of many of God's finest men. This is the second introductory
consideration, the silence of Scripture concerning the death
of many godly men. Both Peter and Paul, two of the strongest
names to be written upon the pages of the New Testament,
pass from the scene without a word concerning their departure.
Tradition holds that Peter was crucified after the manner of
his Lord before him. Tradition also declares that Peter, at
the last moment, requested that his body should be inverted
on the cross, his head pointed toward the earth, because,
tradition declares, he felt himself unworthy to die as his
Lord had before him. But this is tradition, nothing more.
The Scriptural record provides no account of the death of
Peter.

Again, the last Scriptural reference to Paul places him in
bonds in the city of Rome. The traditional view holds that
Paul was executed in Rome, though some continue to believe
that Paul was eventually released and continued his mis-
sionary endeavors, perhaps, in Spain. In any event, the Scriptural record is silent. The Book of Acts concludes with Paul
still a prisoner in Rome.

The death of John the Baptist, or at least the events surrounding his death, is recorded in some detail; yet, the record
contains no words John may have spoken. For long months
John lay in prison. Then came the fateful night when his
death was ordered by the drunken monarch. What was in
the mind of the Baptist as the soldiers approached his cell,

the sword in the hand of the executioner? Did John call for the vengeance of heaven to fall upon the ruthless men who would take his life? Did John call for the judgment of God upon the besotted king who issued the decree of death? The record relates only that his head was brought forth on a "silver charger." We have no word from John.

The silence of the Scriptural record concerning the death of other men surely is not without significance. We suggest it was the purpose of God to direct attention away from the death of other men, so that all our attention might be directed toward that one death which is different from any other. As we listen in the silence, we are doubly gripped by the significance of the words of the dying Savior. Let us pay close attention, then, as we hear Jesus speak the first "word" from the cross, "Father, forgive them, for they know not what they do."

The common, superficial approach to this text is based upon two assumptions, both of which are invalid. First, it is assumed that Jesus was seeking forgiveness for those who were immediately responsible for his death. Second, it is assumed that Jesus' plea was based upon the ignorance of his persecutors. The line of reasoning runs like this: They did not know He was the Son of God. Had they realized who He was, they would not have crucified Him; therefore, their action was taken in ignorance. Thus, the prayer of Christ is interpreted, as though He were seeking their forgiveness on the basis of their ignorance.

If, however, you will give the matter a moment's consideration in the light of your knowledge of the whole of Scripture, you will realize this cannot be true. In terms of the context of the whole Word of God, this simply cannot be the meaning of the prayer of Christ. Why? Because the Scriptures clearly teach that ignorance is not a ground or reason for pardon. In his Epistle to the Romans Paul wrote that no man shall have excuse before God (Rom. 1:20). Those who have heard the gospel, and those who have not heard it — no man shall have excuse before God. Ignorance, therefore, is never ground or reason for pardon.

Ignorance is never an excuse, either before the laws of God or man. Suppose you have been a party to an automobile "accident." When the traffic police arrive to investigate, you may present a variety of excuses. Your vision was obscured; therefore, you did not see the approaching vehicle in time to prevent the collision. You did not realize an icy spot was present on an otherwise dry pavement. The other party to the "accident" was equally at fault. Ah, but your arm was broken in the crash. Nothing can change that fact. The laws of nature, so-called, know no excuse. And what are "natural laws"? They are simply a formulation of the manner in which God usually administers his creation. "Natural law" may be described as a reflection of the very nature of God. After all, God does nothing contrary to his own nature. We readily accept this fact in the physical realm. Scripture indicates that a similar principle obtains in the Scriptural sphere. Ignorance never averts the justice of God.

The manner in which God deals with men, both in his justice and his mercy, may be seen in a comparison of the situation in Sodom and Gomorrah as opposed to that of Nineveh.

Concerning Sodom and Gomorrah, we are given two facts. (1) They were extremely wicked cities. More wicked than other ancient cities? Perhaps not, but extremely wicked nonetheless. (2) They were destroyed by an act of God. In so far as the Scriptural record is concerned, there is no indication that a prophet was sent to call the people of Sodom and Gomorrah to repentance. They sinned, and they were destroyed.

The Biblical record concerning these cities centers about one man, Lot the nephew of Abraham. This one man and his family were permitted to flee the city of Sodom before destruction fell. And their escape is immediately related to the prayer of godly Abraham who "believed, and it was accounted unto Him for righteousness." Were the other residents of Sodom and Gomorrah warned? Were they given opportunity to repent and be spared? Nothing in the record points to a general warning. They sinned, and they died.

By contrast, note God's treatment of the situation at Nineveh. This, too, was an extremely wicked city. We know from the record, by hindsight if you prefer, it was the will of God that Nineveh should be spared at that time. But God did not simply pronounce pardon upon them. This God never does. Instead, God sent the prophet Jonah to preach to the people of Nineveh, to call attention to their sin, to warn them of the wrath of God, and to call them to repentance. The people of Nineveh heard the words of Jonah and repented. Then, and then only, were they granted pardon, and the wrath of God was turned from them.

Thus a principle is set before us. The only pardon known to the Word of God is preceded by repentance. When God wills to grant pardon to the sinner, He first brings the sinner to repentance. This fact is illustrated in the life of King David. Recall the great sin of David, a dual sin involving two heinous crimes, adultery and murder. Again, we can know, it was the will of God that David should be forgiven. But God did not merely pronounce pardon upon David. By no means. God sent the prophet Nathan to accuse David of his sin, to warn David that his sins were known to God, and to call him to repentance. And David did repent! When we hear him cry to God, "Against thee and thee only have I sinned and done that which is evil in thy sight," we know the reality and depth of David's repentance. Then, and then only, after he had repented of his sin, did God pardon David.

When one considers this Scriptural truth, that pardon must always be preceded by repentance, he must perceive immediately that Jesus could not have meant, "Forgive them, because they are ignorant."

What, then, did Jesus ask of God? He asked that those for whom He prayed might be brought to a knowledge of the truth, that conviction of sin might be followed by repentance, and that God would answer their repentance with pardon. Do you not see? Just as when the prophet came to David to bring him to a sense of his sin, so that he pled with God for forgiveness and was forgiven, so we must understand the prayer of Jesus. Jesus would have those for whom He prayed brought to a knowledge of the truth. He would have them to be ignorant of their sin no longer. Rather, they must be convicted of sin that they might be brought to repentance. Then, and not before, they should receive the forgiveness of God.

One cannot doubt that this is the meaning of the prayer of Jesus when he looks upon the crucifixion scene. The scene is not complete, until one has seen, not one cross but three. Beside Jesus hanged the two malefactors, the one on the right hand, the other on the left. Recall, now, that one of the two thieves received pardon from Christ even as he hanged upon the cross. The other remained in his sin and under the condemnation of God's justice. What, then, was the difference between these two? Apparently, these two men were guilty of the same crimes. Each had broken the laws of God and man. Each was receiving the just reward for his crimes against society, dying the death of the cross. Yet one of these men received pardon from God; the other remained under condemnation. Why? Because one repented of his sin; the other did not.

Let us make no mistake then. The prayer of Jesus did not seek pardon for any man on the basis of ignorance or misunderstanding. Jesus prayed, rather, that those for whom He was even then laying down his life might be brought to a knowledge of the truth, that knowledge of the truth would be followed by repentance of their sins, and that through repentance they might receive the pardon of God.

This fact becomes increasingly clear as one considers the identity of those for whom Jesus prayed. Many theories have been advanced on the identity of those for whom Jesus prayed. Some say, Jesus was seeking pardon for the Roman legionnaires who performed the act of crucifying Him. They argue, the soldiers were merely executing orders issued by their superiors. Thus, some contend, they cannot be held responsible for the death of Christ. Others say, Jesus sought pardon for the Jewish rulers who plotted his death. They contend that the members of the Sanhedrin, the chief priests, the scribes, Pharisees, and Sadducees were all religious men who sincerely believed they were putting a blasphemer to death. Had they realized Jesus was the Messiah of prophecy, the argument runs, surely they would not have sought his death. A third explanation holds that Jesus asked pardon for the people of Jerusalem, some of whom had wept as He made His way to Golgotha bearing the weight of the cross. So, it is said, had they only realized who He was, they would not have permitted Him to be crucified. Finally, some continue to hold the universalist interpretation, namely, that Jesus offered this prayer for all men.

None of these suggested interpretations hold validity, because all of them start at the wrong point. The proper point of beginning is to ask, "For whom could Jesus have offered this prayer from the cross?" Only hours earlier He had offered the great high-priestly prayer. Then he had said, "I pray, not for the world but for them whom thou hast given me (John 17:9). From this declaration, and from the context in which it is set, two facts become immediately clear. First, He did not pray for all men. Second, He did pray for some, to wit, those who were given Him by the Father.

Surely this was as true on the cross as it was on the night before his death. After all, He is the same yesterday, today, and forever. Humans frequently change their minds for a variety of reasons, but not God. He is the immutable one, the changeless one. If it be true on the garden path, "I pray, not for the world but for them whom thou hast given me"; it is equally true upon the cross.

The prophecy of Isaiah contains further amplification of this truth. Eight centuries earlier Isaiah wrote, " . . . he hath poured out his soul unto death: and he was numbered with the transgressors" (Isa. 53:12). The reference is clearly to the crucifixion, for we read, "he poured out his soul unto death." Further, we are told the cause of his death, "he was numbered with the transgressors." This is corroborated in the next declaration of the text, "he bare the sin of many." Finally, He "made intercession for the transgressors."

The question becomes, "Who are the transgressors for whom Christ prayed?" To put it another way, He made intercession for the transgressors — but what transgressors? The answer is contained in the verse itself. Consider the two clauses: "He bare the sins of many — and made intercession for the transgressors." The people in each clause are the same. He prayed, hence, for the transgressors whose sins He bore. This is the vital point: He prayed for the trangressors whose sins He bore — for these and none other.

And whose sins did He bear? The sins of "many." Again in the New Testament we read, "He came ... to give his life a ransom for *many*" (Matt. 20:28). Again, "For this is my blood of the new covenant which is shed for *many* for the remission of sins" (Matt. 26:28). Bear in mind, "many" is never "all." The term "many" is indefinite. It might mean a few, or it might mean a multitude, but one thing it does not mean: it assuredly does not mean all men.

Jesus confirmed the limited or particular nature of the atonement when He said, "I am the Good Shepherd, and know my sheep and am known of mine ... and I lay down my life for the sheep" (John 10:14-15). Not for the goats, understand. "I lay down my life for the sheep." More, He tells us that He knows his sheep. Again, John declares, "He calleth his own sheep by name" (John 10:3). Christ died, not for a gray, nameless mass of men but for his own sheep, who are known to Him, and whom He calls by name. For these He also prays. They were given Him by the Father, and He prays, "not for the world but for them whom thou hast given me."

You see, the limits of the prayer of Christ from the cross are defined by the limits of the atonement. It can be no other way. Forgiveness is always grounded in the death of Christ. Apart from Christ and his atoning death, there can be no forgiveness of sins. So now He prayed, "Even as I lay down my life for the sheep, I pray that they may be brought to repentance and faith, and therefore, that they may be forgiven." When they have been forgiven, when they have been turned from death unto life, the prayer of Christ from the cross is fulfilled.

This fact carries numerous implications, blessed, precious implications. The prayer of Christ was offered for every soul who was given to Him by the Father. Abraham, Isaac, Jacob, Moses, to mention but a few — for *their* sins He went to the cross. For you, for me, for all whom He was given by the Father, even from the beginning to the end of time — for these He died, and for these He offered the prayer of the cross.

O, this is meaningful! Neither the atonement nor his prayer from the cross are to be viewed in terms of generalities. He prayed for and He died for those whom He "calls by name." Each of us for himself, all of us collectively as the church which He purchased with the shedding of his blood — we drove the nails into his hands and feet and plunged the spear into his side. No man could impale the Son of God upon the cross. "No man taketh my life. I lay it down of myself." Though God used instruments of wickedness to bring about his death, the primary reason for the death of the cross was, not because wicked men put Him there, but because of those for whom He gave Himself to the death of the cross.

What, then, must this prayer mean to me today, when I realize that my Lord was praying for me even as He hanged upon the cross? He prayed, "Father, forgive them . . . ." I am among "them" for whom He prayed. What, therefore, must this prayer mean to me, "Father, forgive them, for they know not what they do"? He was asking the Father that by his Word and Spirit I might be brought to a knowledge of my sin, that I might be brought to the place of penitence with tears, and also to the place of faith, and therefore, that I might receive from God forgiveness, pardon and the hope of everlasting life and glory.

If one understands the prayer of Christ like this, it becomes a much more tender prayer not only, but a much more personal prayer. When one realizes it was not for a motley little troop of soldiers that Jesus prayed, nor for the rabble rousers of his own day, but for the elect of all ages, for "them whom thou hast given me," and more particularly, for you and for me who now believe on his name, this becomes an intensely personal prayer.

Everyone whom Thou hast given Me, mine own sheep whom I call by name, forgive them, not simply because they are ignorant, but bring them to a knowledge of the truth, bring them to the place of penitence with tears, bring them to the place of the cross, and then forgive them, because I lay down my life for them.

The prayer of Jesus was fulfilled even as He uttered it upon the cross. A moment later the one beside Him pled, "Jesus, Lord, remember me when thou comest into thy kingdom." He replied, "Today, thou shalt be with me in Paradise." A bit later the prayer was fulfilled again, as the centurion looked upward at the crucified Christ and exclaimed, "Truly, this was the Son of God" (Matt. 27:54). The prayer of Christ was fulfilled again on Pentecost Day when Peter preached, "Repent ye, and be baptized, everyone of you in the name of Jesus Christ unto the remission of sins." We read, three thousand souls were added to the church that day (Acts 2:38-41).

The prayer of Jesus is fulfilled among us daily. Whenever one in our number is brought to the place of penitence and confession, this prayer from the lips of Christ is fulfilled. Whenever someone of our number comes to make confession, both of his repentance and his faith, this prayer is fulfilled. Everyone — not merely those who have gone off into the far country of sin and wasted their substance in riotous living.

When we pray for our children, as all of us do, sometimes with many heartaches, knowing that we do not always rightly fulfill our high calling as covenant-keeping parents — we pray, "Create a true faith in the hearts of our children. Hold them in the hollow of thy hand. Never let them go." Long ago, Jesus prayed for everyone whom God has given Him, and He prayed for our children, too, "Father, forgive them . . . ." He prayed in effect: Bring that child to a consciousness of the God-given promise. Bring that child to a realization that we are all corrupt and sinful by nature, that only by grace are we turned to the worship of God and directed to Christ. Bring that child to a realization that into every life must come penitence for sin and faith in Me for redemption and life.

This was the prayer of Jesus on the cross, "Father, forgive them . . . ." I thank God, when He said, "Father, forgive them . . . ," that by faith I may know I was one of the number for whom He prayed. You thank God for that too.

Because he prayed, because the Word and Spirit of God are stronger than the evil in our own breasts and the principalities and powers of darkness around us, because God in his wonderful, matchless, irresistible, sovereign grace has answered the prayer of Christ — that is why you and I worship God in the name of Jesus Christ even now.

2. Converted on a Cross

Verily I say unto thee, Today thou shalt be with me in paradise. — Luke 23:34

Among the most beautiful words in Scripture are those spoken by Christ to the Repentant Thief as each hanged upon his cross at Calvary, "Today thou shalt be with me in paradise." Scripture contains many warm, tender passages. From them the saints have taken comfort, reassurance, courage and hope through the ages. If they should question whether this passage ranks high among them, we might state the proposition like this: If someone you love dearly were but a few hours removed from death, and then, if you could hear the Savior say, "Today thou shalt be with me in paradise," would not these words glow with unusual meaning?

How many of the saints have sought reassurance in their last hours. When death is near one question takes pre-eminence over all others: Is it well with my soul? Then to hear the Lord say, "Today thou shalt be with me in paradise," is surely the fulfillment of the deepest desire of the children of God. Now we shall hear these words spoken from the cross.

We shall not, however, go directly to Calvary. We shall go first to the pages of the Old Testament to look in upon a scene which foreshadows the plea of the Repentant Thief upon the cross. The scene is taken from the life of Joseph. After Joseph had been sold into slavery by his brothers, he was carried into Egypt by slave traders. There, you will recall, he was sold into the household of Potiphar. Soon thereafter his master's wife accused Joseph of crimes he had not committed, and he was cast into prison. This, too, was part of the plan of God for the life of Joseph.

While in prison, Joseph encountered a man who was soon to be released. This fellow was a household servant of the Egyptian monarch. He is known as the king's butler. In the king's butler, Joseph foresaw the possibility of freedom. If this man should find opportunity to present the case of Joseph to the king, Joseph might conceivably be freed. With this in mind, Joseph said to the king's servant, "Remember me, when it is well with thee." Remember me, when you stand before the king. Remember me!

Centuries later, three crosses were implanted upon Calvary's Hill. On the central cross was the Son of God, laying down his life a ransom for many. On either hand were two malefactors who had also been sentenced to the death of the cross. Under these circumstances a conversation took place among the three men, each impaled upon a cross. One of the malefactors sneered, "If thou be Christ, save thyself and us." Jesus did not deign to reply, but the other malefactor did, saying, "Dost thou not fear God, seeing thou art in the same condemnation? And we indeed justly, for we receive the due reward of our deeds, but this man hath done nothing amiss." Then the second malefactor continued, speaking the words which have come ringing down through the ages, "Jesus, Lord, remember me when thou comest into thy kingdom."

Like Joseph, he was asking to be remembered to the end that he might be set free, not from a prison of iron and stone as Joseph was but from the dark dungeon of sin. He had spent a lifetime bound by the chains Satan welds about the souls of men. He was pleading for freedom from the enslaving power of sin, so that he might return to God. The reply of Christ was all he had dared to hope and more, for Jesus said, "Today thou shalt be with me in paradise."

Thus we see a man converted in the very shadow of death. From the reply of Christ we learn that Jesus saw more in the words of the dying thief than meets the natural eye. After all, what do these words mean, "Jesus, Lord, remember me when thou comest into thy kingdom"? From his reply, it is clear, that Jesus found dual meaning in these words. Reading the heart, as only God can, Jesus found in the words of the dying thief both a confession of sin and a profession of faith. Hearing this good confession, both of repentance and of faith, Jesus declared to him, "Today thou shalt be with me in paradise."

For us, several significant factors present themselves in this situation. The first is the reigning providence of God, that is, the government or active direction of God over his creation and of all things contained therein. This the world does not recognize, precisely because spiritual things are spiritually discerned. For unregenerate man, circumstances arise because of chance, fate, coincidence, or at best, by the plan of men. For the child of God, circumstances arise only by the planning and direction of God. And God's direction of all things to their appointed end, we call providence.

Perhaps we shall best discern the action of divine providence, if we ask the question, "What brought these two thieves to be hanged alongside the Son of God?" If one takes the humanistic point of view, mere coincidence placed the cross of the Repentant Thief alongside the cross of Christ. The authorities apparently had no reason for executing this man along with Christ, except that it was convenient to do so. Had this man been captured a day or two earlier, or had he been captured a day or two later, in all probability he would have been executed at another time. Had he been brought to trial a day or two later, in all probability he would have been executed at another time. If someone had asked the officer in charge, "Why are these men being crucified together?" he would have replied, "Because it is simpler to crucify three men together than to crucify them separately."

But the humanistic point of view does not take into consideration the active government of God over his creation. There is no "accident" or "chance" or "happenstance" in the plan of God. Neither is anything done out of mere convenience. Before the worlds were framed, God had ordained that this man should hang upon a cross alongside the Savior. Before the Repentant Thief was born, before he had entered upon a life of crime, before he had been apprehended by the authorities, before Roman justice had required that his life should be terminated upon a cross — before any of these events and circumstances had come to pass, God had ordained that this man should be apprehended at precisely this time, sentence should be pronounced precisely when it was, he should be executed precisely upon this day, and his cross would be erected precisely where it was, that is, alongside the cross of Christ.

Just as Peter was later to declare concerning the death of Christ, He whom "...ye have taken and by wicked hands have crucified and slain..." was "... delivered up by the determinate counsel and foreknowledge of God," so we may say of the Repentant Thief: He whom Roman justice condemned to the death of the cross was actually brought to this time and place by the determinate counsel and foreknowledge of God (Acts 2:23).

Thus we are permitted to view the interplay of the divine and the human. In the instance of the death of Christ, the evil in the hearts of the Jewish rulers caused them to seek the death of our Lord. The corruption in the heart of Judas, the "son of perdition," caused him to betray Christ. A weakness born out of his sinful nature caused Pilate to sentence an innocent man to the cross. Yet, all this came to pass within the framework of the will of God and could not have come to pass had not God foreordained it. So with the Repentant Thief, his own evil nature led him into a life of crime. The Roman authorities had apprehended him and brought him to trial. Now they were executing him; yet, none of this could have come to pass apart from the will of God. God had foreordained that this man should come to this time and to this place where he would be confronted by Christ, even though it be on a cross.

All of us who have been brought into a saving relationship to Christ must view the circumstances of our lives in a similar fashion. Some of us were born into believing, covenant-keeping homes. Through the preaching of the Word in the worship services, through the teaching of the Word in catechetical and Sunday School classes, through the speech and example of our parents, we were brought under the action of the Word and the Spirit of God. Some of us at an earlier age, some of us at a later age came to a personal consciousness both of our sin and of our faith in Christ as our Savior. Then we confessed Him as our Savior and Lord.

Others among us were confronted by Christ in a variety of ways. Some were brought under the preaching of the Word and under the conviction of the Spirit through the relationships developed in courtship and marriage. Others were initially led by friends or associates. One of our elders, a businessman, recently discovered that one of his customers was converted solely through radio preaching. The man had never previously entered the door of a church; yet, he could testify that his life had been changed. He is now a confessing member of a local congregation and busily at work in the life and witness of the church.

Whatever the circumstances in our lives may have been, whether we were reared in the church, whether we were brought into the church by loved ones or friends, or whether we were touched by a radio sermon, we must realize all these circumstances lie within the plan of God for our lives. Just as God directed the course of the Repentant Thief so that his cross was placed alongside the cross of Christ, so He brought each one of us into personal confrontation with Christ.

We must now take a second essential step and view the sovereign grace of God. The providential government of God must not, in itself, be considered a full or complete explanation of this man's conversion experience. This is precisely the point at which many Bible expositors go astray. Many expositors allow the considerations we have noted thus far to stand without further explanation or analysis. Yet this, in itself, is not an explanation for the conversion of the Repentant Thief.

Two malefactors were crucified along with Christ that day. The reigning providence of God brought them both to a cross alongside Christ, the one who remained impenitent, as well as the one who believed. The one turned to Christ in repentance and faith. The other scoffed at Him in disbelief of his Savior-hood. How shall one explain it? Why did one repent of his sin, while the other died in his sin? Why did one turn to Christ in faith, while the other turned from Him in unbelief?

It is commonly held that they were of comparable age and of similar background and experience. Both are believed to have been of Jewish stock, since a Roman citizen would not have been crucified. Apparently the two malefactors were well acquainted with each other. They also possessed more than passing knowledge of Jesus. This becomes apparent from the conversational interchange among them. While the one scoffed at the Saviorhood of Jesus, the other could say, " . . . we [are here] justly, for we receive the due reward of our deeds, but this man hath done nothing amiss." This much is certain: Both had committed capital crimes. Now both were dying the death of the cross. So much these two had in common; yet, one turned to Christ in faith, while the other from Him in unbelief. Again we ask: How shall one explain it?

It must be explained in the same way as every other instance of conversion set forth in the Word of God. This is true, because Scripture sets forth but one great principle of salvation. Paul enunciated it when he wrote, "By grace are ye saved, through faith; and that not of yourselves: it is the gift of God: Not of works, lest any man should boast" (Eph. 2:8-9) . The faith of the Repentant Thief, therefore, must be viewed as the gift of God, implanted in his heart as the result of divine favor.

When we think of these two men, hanging upon their crosses, the one in faith, the other in unbelief, we should think immediately of two other men, Jacob and Esau. They were, of course, twin brothers and, therefore, had much in common; yet, as we read the Old Testament record, we learn one became a man of faith, while the other remained in unbelief. Not until we read Paul's Epistle to the Romans, however, do we perceive the underlying cause in the decretive will of God. In the ninth chapter of Romans we read, " . . . the children being not yet born, neither having done anything good or evil, that the purpose of God according to election might stand, not of works but of Him that calleth, it was said unto [the mother] . . . Jacob have I loved, but Esau have I hated" (Rom. 9:11-13). "So then," concluded Paul, "it is not of him that willeth, nor of him that runneth, but of God who showeth mercy" (9:16).

Now do you perceive why one thief believed while the other scoffed? Not of him that willeth, nor of him that runneth, but of God who showeth mercy! So God wrought his purposes in the lives of these two men, just as God executes his sovereign purpose in the lives of all men. When Paul preached to the people of Pisidian Antioch, some believed while others did not, and this is what we read by way of explanation, "As many as were ordained unto eternal life believed" (Acts 13:48). We must realize that the Repentant Thief was ordained unto eternal life; therefore, he believed. Again, Paul preached to a group of women who were gathered on the banks of the river at Philippi. Out of that group of women, one believed. Her name, of course, was Lydia. Why did Lydia believe while the others did not? We read, "The Lord opened her heart, so that she attended to the things which were spoken by Paul" (Acts 16:14). So the Lord "opened the heart" of the malefactor, causing him to repent and believe.

You see, we sometimes fail to plumb the spiritual depths of the conversion of the Repentant Thief. Two explanations are commonly offered for the conversion of the Repentant Thief. The first is that the excruciating pain of the cross caused him to consider spiritual values as he had never done before. The second and closely related explanation is that the approach of death brought him to a realization of his lost spiritual condition. We readily acknowledge that both of these elements were factors in his conversion. His pain and the realization that death was near undoubtedly had some bearing upon his conversion. We may say, quite correctly, these were external instruments in the hand of God.

We must realize, however, that neither pain nor fear of death were sufficient in themselves to bring about his conversion. If either pain or fear of death were sufficient in themselves to bring about the conversion of man, the other male-factor would also have been converted. External forces will never, in themselves, bring about the conversion of man. External forces may be used of God toward conversion, to be certain, but conversion results when, and only when, God does an internal work of grace within the heart of man. We must say of the Repentant Thief, therefore, even as it was said of Lydia, "The Lord opened [his] heart...."

In paying heed to this fact, we acknowledge that all glory belongs unto the Lord in our own salvation. We also take hope concerning the salvation of our loved ones and others to whom we bear witness. How often has a godly father re-marked of a wayward son, "I don't know what more I can say or do." How many godly parents have spoken these dis-heartening words! Take hope, however, for God may yet work the miracle of redeeming grace in the heart of your son or daughter, as the case may be.

How long should you take hope? As long as the breath of life remains within their bodies. This is the comforting lesson of the Repentant Thief upon the cross: God may yet work the miracle of redeeming grace in the heart of man, even as he stands in the very shadow of death. If you are doing your best with someone you love, continue to do it. And do one more thing, continue to pray that God will work the miracle of grace in the heart of the one you love.

We must remember, too, God works in his own good time to the accomplishment of his purposes. Missionaries of the gospel live daily with this fact across the world. We must likewise learn to accept it as we work with our loved ones and those about us. Sometimes the missionaries work for many years in a particular field before gaining a single convert. Again, in another field, they will bring the gospel message, and many conversions will result almost immediately. There-fore, just as our missionaries must learn, not only to pray but to wait upon the Lord, so we must learn, not only to pray but to wait upon the Lord.

Before we dismiss this aspect of the subject, however, we must speak a word to those who have not yet come to the place of confession. Some may have delayed for a little time, some for many years. Perhaps you are like the other thief. His eyes were so blind, his ears so deaf, his heart so hard that he turned away from Christ even as he stood in the shadow of death. If this is your condition, if you will not hear the gospel, if you will not be moved to repentance and faith by the sight of the dying Savior, if your hardened heart will not respond, nothing remains to be said. Jesus said of such in the days of his ministry, "Ye will not come unto me that ye might have life" (John 5:40).

If, on the other hand, the Spirit of God is speaking to your soul, even though it be but a still, small voice, we must urge you not to delay but to bow before the Christ of the cross in contrition and faith. You must not take false comfort in the conversion of the Repentant Thief. Consider what God did to this man to bring him to repentance and faith. God nailed him to a cross in order to convert him! God brought him to a cross where the nails were driven into his hands and feet in order that he might be brought to repentance and faith.

What, then, must God do in your life to bring you to the place of confession? Must God crush your body in order to prevail upon your soul? Must God bring pain and suffering into your life, as He did into the life of the Repentant Thief, in order to bring you to your knees? Must God remove a loved one, bringing death and mourning into the circle of your family, in order to bring you to the place of penitence with tears? O, if God is determined to have you, He will bring you to your knees, but consider what terrible thing must God do in your life in order to make you cry out, "Jesus Lord, remember me when thou comest into thy kingdom"?

Consider also the reply of Christ to the Repentant Thief. Jesus said "Today, thou shalt be with me in paradise." These were beautiful words to the Repentant Thief. They continue to be beautiful words for every child of God. They tell us two things. First, they speak to us of God's abundant mercy. No one has ever sinned so deeply but that his sin may be covered in the blood of Christ. To those who fear they have sinned too grievously to be forgiven, we may say: Look at this man upon his cross. His sins were such, they had brought him to the death of the cross, but God forgave him there. You, too, may have sinned grievously in the sight of God. You may have refused to worship God. You may have profaned his holy name. You may have desecrated the Lord's day. You may have violated the holy institution of marriage. You may have committed adultery. You may have committed murder. You need not necessarily despair. God is able to cleanse the vilest sins in the blood of Christ. This is the word of gladness, "Though your sins be as scarlet, they shall be white as snow."

Again, to all who believe, the words of Christ are beautiful, because they speak of the future state and condition of the redeemed soul. "Today" — the very day you die, the very day your soul departs your body — "thou shalt be with me in paradise." Not in that never, never land called Purgatory which is utterly foreign to the Word of God, but "with me in paradise." It is almost inconceivable that multitudes are living under a shadow now, in the latter half of the twentieth century, because they have been taught that their departed loved ones are enduring the tortures of a fictitious Purgatory.

The argument runs something like this: A very righteous man may be permitted to enter the place of blessedness and dwell with God, but most men have sins which must be paid for and cleansed after they die. They ask, "How can a sinful man enter into the presence of God?" Ah, but what of the Repentant Thief? If ever a man had sinned grievously, it was this man upon the cross. His were not little or "venial" sins. His were the most vicious and terrible crimes known to man, so vicious, so terrible that justice demanded the death of the cross. If there were a Purgatory, if ever there were a man who should have been sentenced to it, this was the man; yet, Jesus said, "Today thou shalt be with me in paradise."

This teaches us, as does the whole of Scripture, that forgiveness in Christ is both sufficient and final. Nothing more, absolutely nothing more, is necessary. There is no need for further sacrifice. There is no need for further cleansing. In the words of Scripture, " . . . the blood of Jesus Christ, his Son, cleanseth us from *all* sin" (I John 1:7).

I thank God that I need never say to a grieving family, "My dear friends, your departed loved one is now in Purgatory, suffering the torments of the damned." It is not my prerogative to pass judgment upon the souls of men. It is not for me to suggest that one who has departed is either in heaven or in hell, but I can know and I do know, these are the only alternatives. There is no place between. So I may stand with the loss-stricken family, and if their loved one has been found faithful to the end, we may say of him, even as Christ said to the Repentant Thief, "Today thou shalt be with me in paradise."

3. Union and Communion

Woman, behold thy son! . . . Behold thy mother!
—John 19:26, 27

An article in a religious journal discussed the question of whom it was that suffered the more: Jesus as He hanged upon the cross, or the mother of Jesus who stood at the foot of the cross, witnessing her son die a criminal death. Perhaps such speculation appeals to the sentimental strain which all of us possess in greater or lesser degree, but it is evidence of a fatal misunderstanding of the nature of the atonement. To suggest a comparison between the suffering of the Savior and that of Mary, as his mother after the flesh, is to ignore one of the fundamental facts of the death of Christ. Jesus, in taking upon Himself the guilt of sinful men, suffered as none other ever suffered or could suffer. No mere man could have borne the wrath of God against the sins of the world. Only the Son of God, infinite in his own being, could suffer the infinite wrath of God upon the sins of men.

Even so, one cannot dismiss the fact that Mary must have suffered as only a mother can, as she stood at the foot of the cross. The love of a mother for her child is unlike that of any other. No son has ever committed a deed so vile but that his mother loved him still. A man's wife may divorce him. A man's children may turn against him. His friends may neglect him. His neighbors may ostracize him. But his mother will love him still. This is the reason only a mother can fully appreciate what lay in the heart of Mary as she stood at the foot of the cross on which her first born Son was crucified.

Then Jesus spoke to Mary. This was his first word to those who stood at the foot of the cross. Previously He had lifted his eyes heavenward to offer the great intercessory prayer, "Father, forgive them, for they know not what they do." Then he had turned to the malefactor who occupied the cross along- side Him to say, "Today, thou shalt be with me in paradise." Now his eyes turned downward to the earth in which the cross had been planted. He had no need to scan the faces of the multitude surrounding the cross in order to locate his mother. She stood precisely where one would expect a mother to stand, at the very foot of the cross, almost touching his nail-pierced foot. Beside Mary stood John, the beloved apostle. Looking upon these two together Jesus said, "Woman, behold thy son," and to the disciple, "Behold thy mother."

This "word" has been variously designated as the word of "tenderness," the word of "concern," the word of "comfort," the word of "compassion" — to mention but a few. Each of these titles points to an aspect of the truth conveyed in the third "word" from the cross; yet, none of them points to the root concept out of which all other considerations arise. The first key to the third word from the cross is to be found in the form of address Jesus employed as he spoke to his mother. How does a son normally address the woman who brought him into the world? He usually calls her "mother," does he not?

If we may digress for a moment, are you not disturbed when you hear a son address his father by his given name, or a daughter address her mother by her given name? Some parents encourage this practice on the theory that this is a means to- ward achieving a closer relationship with their children. This is an absurd theory. The end result is to destroy the respect children ought rightly to have for their parents. Children, ac- cording to the Scriptures, are to honor their parents. Let a man be a friend to his son, but let him be a father first of all. Let a woman be a friend to her daughter, but let her be a mother first of all. It is right to address our parents as "father" and "mother."

Precisely because this is so, we expect to hear Jesus address Mary as "mother." We are startled for a moment to hear Him address Mary simply as woman — "Woman, behold thy son." This is not a mistranslation, nor should it be ascribed either to haste or pain. We make these assertions, because expositors have long sought to temper the fact that Jesus addressed Mary simply as "woman." Some return to the word in the original language, *gunai*, and point out that the term "woman" bore different connotations in its ancient usage than it does among us today. Extensive word studies have been made to demonstrate that Jesus intended no disrespect toward Mary.

Of course, Jesus intended no disrespect toward Mary! He ever taught men to honor their parents, and He did no less Himself. At the same time, such strenuous efforts to demonstrate that Jesus intended no disrespect for Mary imply a failure to grasp the intent and purpose of Jesus in speaking to Mary as He did. What was his purpose in thus addressing Mary? He was pointing to a basic spiritual truth, namely, there is a higher order of relationships than that of flesh and blood. Indeed, flesh and blood relationships can never be more than temporal and earthly. Only spiritual relationships can be permanent and heavenly. Therefore, only spiritual relationships have abiding value.

The earthly relationship between Jesus and Mary would soon terminate. The tie of flesh and blood would soon be dissolved. Soon his blessed body would be laid to rest in the tomb. When He came forth on the third day, He would arise in the "resurrection" body. The "natural body" was laid in the tomb, but a "spiritual body" came forth on the third day (I Cor. 15:44). In this connection Paul wrote, "Behold, I show you a mystery; we shall not all sleep, but we shall all be changed . . . ." Why? Because ". . . flesh and blood cannot inherit the kingdom of God . . ." (I Cor. 15:50-51). For us this remains a great "mystery," even as the apostle said. For Jesus, as the "firstfruits" of them that shall rise and as an "earnest" of that which is to come, this would become a reality in three days.

We would wear the cloak of flesh and blood no more. But Mary must neither sorrow nor despair. A higher bond, an unbreakable bond, lay between them. This was the spiritual bond which should unite them throughout eternity. Thus, far from demonstrating disrespect for Mary, Jesus was, rather, comforting her with the only true comfort, that is, by imparting knowledge of spiritual truth. Earlier, in seeking to comfort his disciples, He had said, "I will pray the Father and he shall give you another Comforter .... Even the Spirit of truth" (John 14:16-17). Now He comforted Mary with truth, the truth of a higher order of relationships which abides forever.

Mary should not be thought unusual or imperceptive, if she failed to grasp this fact immediately, even though He had sought to teach her this truth much earlier. Jesus had used the term "woman" in addressing his mother upon another occasion. At the beginning of his public ministry, one may see Jesus at the marriage celebration in Cana. At Cana, you will recall, the supply of wine began to run low. Jesus was among the guests. Mary was also present, apparently in a role beyond that of a mere guest, for she came hurriedly to Jesus to explain the situation. When she did, Jesus said to her, "Woman, what have I to do with thee ... ?" Note, again, Jesus addressed the woman who had served as his channel of entry into the world, not as "mother" but as "woman."

From this prior use of the term "woman" may be deduced a second reason for Jesus' use of this form of address. He used the term "woman" to avoid any presumption on the part of Mary or others. Mary was not unacquainted with the uniqueness of her child. The angel had said to her, "The Holy Ghost shall come upon thee, and the power of the most high shall overshadow thee; therefore, the holy thing which shall be born of thee shall be called the Son of God" (Luke 1:35). Further, the very fact that Mary should come to Jesus with her problem at the wedding celebration implies that she was already acquainted with his supernatural powers. Even so, Mary apparently viewed Jesus, in some measure at least, as other mothers view their sons. She came to Him, apparently expecting He would do her bidding.

Jesus replied, "Woman, what have I to do with thee?" Though no disrespect of Mary's motherhood was implied in this form of address, surely Jesus did intend that she should be reminded of her place. Mary had indeed been highly favored of God. God had chosen her to become the instrument whereby the Eternal Son would come into the world. To this end, she had been richly blessed of grace, so that she might fulfill the unusual place accorded to her in the plan of God. But Mary must not forget her place! She is an instrument of God. As an instrument of God, she must not presume that divine favor carries with it the presumptive right to dictate to the Son of God.

Perhaps Jesus was thinking more of those who would come after Mary in succeeding generations than He was of Mary herself. Official Roman theology makes the error of presumption which is implied in Mary's speech at Cana. Rome speaks of Mary as the "mother of God," rather than as the woman from whom the Second Person of the Trinity took his flesh and blood. Then Roman theology takes a second step, which is, to presume that Mary can dictate to or at least prevail upon the Eternal Son of God. Thus, members of the church of Rome are taught to pray to Mary, so that she may prevail upon Christ to answer human prayers.

This not only indicates a serious misunderstanding of the place and function of Mary in the plan of God, but it must ultimately lead to an idolatrous view of Mary. We do not seek to belittle Mary; by no means. We do not fail to recognize her function as an instrument of God, highly favored and endowed of grace, but we must not ascribe to her a position no mere human can occupy nor a power no mere human can possess; and therefore, we must not worship her, nor idolize her, nor venerate her. We do well to remember the words of Christ which put an end to all presumptuousness, "Woman, what have I to do with thee?"

To return to the basic consideration, when Jesus addressed Mary from the cross, "Woman, behold thy son," He displayed, as always He did, a divine insight into the only abiding relationship between a mother and her son, and for that matter, the true nature of the relationship between all believers. What is the nature of this relationship? It is spiritual. The most basic relationships in life are spiritual, not those of flesh and blood.

More specifically, what is the true nature of our spiritual relationships? They are two-fold. The first or prior relationship is that which we have to Christ. Theologians refer to it as "union with Christ" or sometimes as "mystical union." Jesus said, "In that day [when all things are made plain] ye shall know that I am in my Father, and ye in me, and I in you" (John 14:20). The apostle Paul wrote, "I am crucified with Christ; nevertheless, I live; yet not I, but Christ liveth in me..." (Gal. 2:20). Nor must Paul's statement be taken as a mere figure of speech but as a living reality, the Spirit of Christ living within the believer.

Our Lord set forth the figure of the vine and the branches. He said, "I am the vine. Ye are the branches" (John 15:5). So essential is this relationship that He added, "Without me, ye can do nothing" (John 15:5). Again, the apostle spoke of this relationship in terms of the various members of the human body. Paul described Christ as the "head" (Eph. 1:22-23) of the body and wrote further, "So we, being many, are one body in Christ, and everyone members one of another" (Rom. 12:5). Still again, the apostle spoke of the relationship between Christ and his church, that is, between Christ and the body of believers, as comparable to the relationship between husband and wife (Eph. 5:23).

Our primary relationship, therefore, is the close, intimate relationship which we enjoy with our Lord. The second relationship develops out of the first. Each branch is related to every other which is attached to the vine, precisely because they are all rooted in the same vine. They have a common source of life in the vine. They have one life, because they are rooted in one vine.

Again, we are related to each other as members of one Body, the Body of Christ. This figure presents an added facet of the nature of our relationship to each other. Our relationship to each other as members of one Body is such that each member of the Body is affected in some degree by the condition of every other (I Cor. 12:26; Heb. 13:3). If the eye is injured, for example, the entire body is made miserable by the affliction of the eye. If the palate is pleased by a choice morsel of food, the entire body participates in the pleasure.

While these figures are instructive, still another is, perhaps, more appealing. It is the figure of the family. We are related to the Father and to our Elder Brother, the first born of many brethren (Rom. 8:29), as members of one family, the family of God. In Christ we become the children of God. As the children of God, we are brothers and sisters to each other. This is the essential nature of our confession when we say, "I believe in . . . the communion of the saints." We have an essential and integral relationship together, because we are members of one family, the family of God.

All this is further illustrated in another incident from the life of Christ. One day Jesus was addressing a group when his mother and brothers appeared. Apparently they were hidden from Jesus' view by the people who surrounded Him as He talked. Because He was God as well as man, He must have known they were present, even though they were hidden from his view, but He took no recognition of them. Then one of the disciples came to Him with the message, "Behold, thy mother and thy brethren stand without, seeking to speak to thee." Jesus replied, "Who is my mother? And who are my brethren? . . . Whosoever shall do the will of my Father who is in heaven, he is my brother and sister and mother" (Matt. 12:46-50). Jesus was saying, in effect, that flesh and blood are not the basic factors which bind two people together. Two people must be joined in the bonds of the Spirit, or in the deepest sense, they are not joined at all.

Admittedly, many things may serve as temporal bonds between two people. Two men may be brought together temporally, because they mutually enjoy hunting, fishing, bowling, or golf. Two people may be drawn together temporally, because they enjoy the same books, the same music, or perhaps, the same radio and television programs. Indeed, two people may be brought together temporally by liquor; they become drinking companions. Note, however, that we have consistently used the qualifying adjective "temporal" and the modifying adverb "temporally." Such bonds as these are transitory. At most, they form a bond which is limited to earth and time. The only permanent bonds, the only eternal bonds are those which we form within the body of Christ.

Would to God that our young people should become impressed by this fact. How often a young man or a young woman will say of a prospective mate, "We have so many things in common together." Do you now? Do you have so many things in common? To you I would put but one question: Do you have Christ in common? Does this young man, this young woman worship God? The same God whom you worship? Is he, is she, joined to Christ in the bonds of a true faith? If this is not true, you have nothing in common — for eternity. All other bonds are limited to earth and time. Only one bond transcends the world. Only one bond stretches out into eternity, the bond which we have in Christ.

In the highest sense, Mary could be a mother to Jesus, because she was a child of God, and therefore, because she did the will of his Father in heaven. Speaking hypothetically for a moment, had not Mary been a child of God, had she not done the will of our Father in heaven, she could have had no relationship to Christ, much less could she have been a mother to Him.

One of our human errors lies in the stress we place on mere flesh and blood relationships. In the Scriptures we learn that two men may be brothers in terms of flesh and blood, but at the same time, they may be separated by a great gulf spiritually. Cain and Abel were brothers in terms of the flesh. Though the same blood flowed through their veins, one brother slew the other. What lay basic to their separation? One was a child of God; the other was not. Therefore, though they were brothers in terms of flesh and blood, they were unrelated, even enemies, in terms of the spirit.

Jacob and Esau were flesh and blood brothers; yet, two men could scarcely have been more unlike each other. They were so unlike each other, they could find no fellowship together. As boys, one played in the fields; the other preferred to remain at his mother's side. As men, they lived far removed from each other, not only geographically but, more important, spiritually. Why? Basically, because one was a child of God who learned, even though only later in life, to do the will of our Father in heaven, while the other was a reprobate, alienated from God and in rebellion against God.

Thirdly, none of this should be taken to imply that Jesus lacked affection for his mother. To the contrary, we know He loved her. Ah, yes, but why? Because she had served as the instrument of God to bring Him into the world? Because He was bone of her bone and flesh of her flesh? To this we must answer: Only as these things are related to a more fundamental fact, namely, that Mary was a child of God, holding in her heart a true faith, and doing the will of the Father. Jesus said, "She is my mother who does the will of my Father in heaven." And Mary did the will of the Father; therefore, she could be the mother of Christ.

The highest compliment Jesus paid to Mary came in the words He spoke from the cross. John was very dear to Jesus. When Jesus said, "Woman, behold thy son," and to John, "Behold thy mother," He was saying that these two were mother and son to each other, because both were members of the same family, the family of God. Had not Mary been a child of God, Jesus could not have said to her, "Woman, behold thy son," for John was a child of God. Again, had not John been a child of God, Jesus could not have said, "Behold thy mother," for these two would have had no common bond to draw them together. They were mother and son to each other, because both were the children of God.

In the final analysis all men are members of either of two families. Jesus said of some, "Ye are of your father, the devil . . ." (John 8:44). By contrast, John wrote, "As many as received him, to them gave he power to become the sons of God, even to them that believe on his name, who were born,

not of blood, nor of the will of the flesh, nor of the will of
man, but of God" (John 1:12-13) . Spiritually, a man is either
the son of God or the son of Satan. The population of the
earth is ultimately divided into two great families: the elect
family of God, and the reprobate family of Satan. Those who
serve the Lord are the sons of God. Those who continue to
serve the world, the flesh, and the devil are the sons of Satan.
John and Mary were related to each other, indeed were members of the same family, because both were children of God.

One day Jesus came upon a young man to whom He said,
"Follow me." The young man replied, "I will follow after
thee, Lord, but first I must bury my father." Jesus replied,
"Let the dead bury their dead, but go thou and preach the
gospel" (Luke 9:59-60) . The reply of Jesus may appear harsh
at first. He ordered a young man to leave his aged father. But
consider: If this young man served God and his father did not,
then they were not father and son at all. The one belonged to
the redeemed family of God. The other belonged to the reprobate family of Satan. Though they were of the same flesh and
blood, these two were not really related at all.

Again Jesus said, "I have come, not to bring peace but a
sword, for I have come to separate a father from a son and a
mother from a daughter . . . and a man's foes shall be they of
his own household" (Matt. 10:34-36) . That is to say, when a
father serves God but a son does not, or when a son serves
God but a father does not, they are not really father and son
at all. When a mother serves God but her daughter does not,
or a daughter serves God but her mother does not, they are
not really mother and daughter. They are members of two
different families. The one who serves God is a member of
the family of God. The other is a member of the family of
Satan.

Admittedly, we cannot pre-judge these situations. Our Lord
could say, "Ye are of your father, the devil," because He could
read the heart of man. This we cannot do. As long as we remain in the world, therefore, we can both hope and pray that
a loved one who remains enslaved by sin may yet, by the
intervention of divine grace, become a child of God. Only in

eternity shall we discover where the family lines are drawn. Then we shall know but not before.

One day a question was raised in the Sunday School by a woman who asked, "Won't we be uncomfortable in heaven, if members of our own families are absent?" The answer is: Not at all. The glass through which we now see but darkly shall then be removed. We shall know even as we are known. Then the redeemed will clearly realize that any unsaved member of their family was not truly a member of the same family at all, but a member of an entirely different family, the family of Satan.

Fourthly, we should perceive in the words of Jesus the self-sacrificing character of the redemptive love of God. We are aware of this fact in a general way. We know the love of God is of such character that He "spared not his own Son but delivered him up for us all." We know, too, that the Son of God gave Himself freely to the death of the cross. He could say, "No man taketh my life; I lay it down of myself. I have power to lay it down and power to take it up again" (John 10:18).

Now, however, we are permitted to witness a specific example of the self-sacrificing character of the redemptive love of God. Consider the scene at Calvary. In a few moments He will cry, "My God, my God, why hast thou forsaken me?" testifying to the unspeakable agony through which we must pass as the desolation of the wrath of God comes upon Him. After a bit, He will also emit the seemingly pitiful plea, "I thirst," reflecting his intense suffering of body and soul. Before He permits Himself to think of his own condition, however, his concern is for those whom He loves. Before He permits the excruciating agony of body and soul to envelop Him, He must make provision for those whom He loves, "Woman, behold thy son. . . . Behold thy mother."

Why? Why this solicitude for Mary? Because He had received his flesh and blood from this woman? We have already shown that flesh and blood relationships can never be primary or abiding. What, then, was the reason for his solicitude? Mary had been given to Him. This is the basic consideration. Perhaps someone is thinking we have the matter reversed.

Perhaps someone is thinking, "Christ was given to Mary, not Mary to Christ." If you are thinking that He was given to her as a babe in Bethlehem, you are quite correct, but you must not disregard a prior fact: Mary was given to Christ from eternity. Her testimony was, "My spirit hath rejoiced in God *my Savior*" (Luke 1:47). She was numbered among those for whom He prayed when He said, "I pray not for the world but for them whom thou hast given me" (John 17:9). Mary was numbered with those of whom He spoke to the Father saying, "I kept them in thy name; those that thou gavest me I have kept, and none of them is lost, but the son of perdition, that the Scripture might be fulfilled" (John 17:12). From eternity, Mary had been given to Christ.

With the same solicitude which Jesus demonstrated for Mary and John as the children of God, with the same self-sacrificing, redemptive love, He loves each one of us who know by faith that we are numbered among the children of God. We have an High-Priest, even the ascended Christ, who is "touched with the feeling of our infirmity." He knoweth our frame, that we are as dust. In our weakness, in our frailty, in our sorrows and tears, He looks upon us and loves us — not because we are worthy of His love, but because we belong to Him.

From eternity He covenanted with the Father that, in return for his perfect life and atoning death, He would be given an elect people, a royal priesthood, drawn out of every tongue and tribe and nation. We were given to Him. We are his possession; therefore, He has redeemed us unto Himself not only, but He guides our footsteps along the way, ever watching over us, even as He watched over Mary and John from the cross.

When we sin, He sends his Word and Spirit into our hearts that we may sorrow over our sin and repent of it. When our faith wavers, He who is the Author and the Finisher of our faith causes faith to wax strong in our hearts once again. When we would be unfaithful to our God, he sanctifies our lives, so that we may truly seek first the kingdom of God in all things.

What more would you ask, beloved?

> "All the way our Savior leads us,
> What have we to ask beside?
> Can we doubt his tender mercy,
> Whom through life has been our guide?
> Heavenly peace, divinest comfort,
> Here by faith in Him to dwell,
> For we know whate'er betide us,
> Jesus doeth all things well."

When, therefore, you hear Him say, "Woman, behold thy son.... Behold thy mother," be assured, he holds the same self-sacrificing, redemptive love for each of us who were given to Him from eternity, who are heirs and joint heirs along with Christ, and who await the day of his appearing.

4. The Death of the Second Adam

My God, my God, why hast thou forsaken me.—Matt. 27:46

When Martin Luther preached upon the fourth word from the cross, "My God, my God, why hast thou forsaken me?" he is reputed to have exclaimed, "God forsaken of God! Who can understand it?" If this were an accurate description of the climax of Calvary, it would indeed lie beyond human understanding. As Martin Luther well knew, however, the Crucified One was, not only "very God of very God" but "very man of very man." Jesus could utter this cry, precisely because He was as truly man as He was truly God. Thus Martin Luther pointed to an essential fact of the person and work of Christ, namely, his Godhead and his humanity. On the one hand, the Savior of men could be nothing less than true God. On the other, He could be nothing less than true man.

Why must the Savior be true man? Because, replies a well-known catechism, "God will not punish any other creature for the sin which man has committed ..." (Heidelberg, Q. 14). Again this same catechism declares, "... the justice of God requires that the same human nature which hath sinned should likewise make satisfaction for sin ..." (Heidelberg, Q. 16). All the sacrifices performed in the Old Testament era could not make propitiation for the sin of man. The sin of man cannot be punished in an animal. The Old Testament sacrifices could only point to the Lamb of God who would make the one sacrifice which could pay the price of sin. And He whom we know as the Lamb of God could make that one sacrifice which would satisfy the justice of God once and forever, because He was man. Man had sinned. Only man could make satisfaction for sin.

At the same time, the Savior must be true God. Why? "That He might, by the power of his Godhead, sustain in his human nature the burden of God's wrath . . ." (Heidelberg, Q. 17). Always we must see in the person of Christ these two co-existent realities, his true Godhead and his true humanity, but nowhere is the necessity more evident than in the darkest hours of the atonement. Man must bear this fearful burden, unless He be the God-man whose very Godhead would sustain his humanity as the fearful wrath of God against sin was vented upon Him.

We have called the experience which wrought the cry, "My God, my God, why hast thou forsaken me?" the "climax of Calvary." We do so, because this experience, being forsaken of the Father, cut off from God, stands at the heart and center of the atonement. Apparently this fact is not clear to all. Many sermons, many books, many commentaries leave the impression that the physical death which Christ experienced upon the cross, in and of itself, constituted the atonement. We must understand, therefore, that his physical death was but one aspect of the atonement. At the heart of the atonement stands his spiritual death, the fact that He was cut off from God.

Perhaps this fact will become evident, if we return to the time of man's innocence in the paradise garden of Eden. In the time of creation, God entered into covenant with man (Hosea 6:7 ASV). This, the first of the covenants with man, is commonly called the "covenant of works" or the "covenant of life." The terms of the covenant are usually stated like this: If man would live righteously before his God, he would be granted immortality. If, on the other hand, man should sin against his God, he would surely die.

One may, however, draw inaccurate inferences from this statement of the "covenant of works." The covenant of works was neither mechanical, external nor legalistic in essence. At the heart of the covenant lay the first and great command-ment. Man must love his God with all his heart, with all his mind, with all his soul, and with all his strength. If man should live righteously before the face of his God, this would demonstrate his love toward God. If man should sin against God, his sin would demonstrate his lack of love for God. This man did, as well we know. He sinned against his God. Thus he demonstrated, not that he loved God but that he hated God. This was the action of the "First Adam." He sinned against his God and thereby incurred the death penalty.

Now we must ask a question. When God forewarned Adam that sin would result in death, what did this mean to Adam? Death could scarcely have had the same meaning for Adam which it has for us. When death is mentioned, we immediately form certain mental images. With the mention of death, we think of the still form of a loved one, of the hospital, of the frantic efforts of doctors and nurses, and later, of the funeral caravan and the resting place of the dead. All these images, clearly, are related to physical death, the departure of the soul of man, the dissolution of the body.

Ah, but what did the term "death" mean to Adam when God said, "Thou shalt surely die"? Adam had never witnessed physical death, as we have in the lives of our loved ones. Adam had never attended a funeral service, as we do from time to time. Adam had never experienced illness, much less death. Adam lived in a world without a cemetery. For Adam, therefore, death did not evoke the mental imagery which it does for us. To put it another way, Adam was not preconditioned so that the term "death" would mean for him what it does for us.

What, then, did "death" mean to Adam? What was his understanding when God said, "If thou shalt sin, thou shalt surely die"? For Adam, death meant precisely what God intended it should mean, separation from God. God said to Adam, in effect, "If thou shalt sin, our fellowship together shall be broken. We can no longer have communion, walking together in the garden in the cool of the day. You will be cut off from me." This is the basic, Biblical meaning of death — to be cut off, to be separated from God.

He who is separated from God becomes like the branch which has been broken off from the vine. The branch must wither and die, because it has been cut off from the source of its life in the vine. So man, when he is cut off from God, is cut off from the source of his life. The result is death, not physical death first of all, you understand, but spiritual death, death in trespasses and sin.

Consider, too, what came to pass when Adam and Eve sinned against God. God had said, "Thou shalt surely die"; yet, they were not struck to the ground. Physically, they seemed untouched, at least for the moment. Their hearts continued to beat within their breasts. Though they were excluded from the garden, they continued to dwell upon the earth. They lived and worked and bore children. What shall we say then? Shall we conclude that God's word to them was void? Was his threat of death an empty one? Shall we conclude that Adam and Eve paid no penalty for their sin against God? Not so! God's dire warning was fulfilled, not a year later, nor a week later, nor an hour later but immediately. In the very moment of their sin, instantaneously, death struck. In that very moment, they were cut off from God.

Prior to their sin, Adam and Eve inhabited the paradise garden where they basked in the fellowship of God. After their sin, they were expelled from the garden and never permitted to re-enter. Again, prior to their sin, they enjoyed intimate communion with God. The Scriptures describe the relationship between man and his God in these words, "Adam walked with God in the garden in the cool of the day." With Adam's sin, his communion with God was ruptured. Never again does one read that Adam walked with God. There was no more walking with God, no more communion with God, no more fellowship with God. Death had come; Adam had been separated from God by his sin.

This is the deeper meaning, the spiritual meaning of death. Indeed, this is death! If this be true, however, what then is the nature of the experience commonly called death? To state the question somewhat differently, what is the relationship between spiritual death and physical death? Physical death may be described as an external manifestation of an inner spiritual condition. One might describe physical death as a symptom of the real problem, namely, spiritual death.

Perhaps a homely illustration will prove helpful. We use a clinical thermometer to determine the degree of body temperature. A rising temperature warns us that an infection is present. This is important, but we are not deceived as to the nature of the problem. The rising temperature is not the problem. It is merely a symptom which warns us that a problem is present. The problem is the infection which causes the body temperature to rise. In much the same fashion, physical death, the departure of the soul from the body and the subsequent dissolution of the body, is a symptom of the root condition, which is, separation from God. Physical death is, therefore, a sign. It tells us something is wrong with man, something is terribly wrong, and that something is the condition which exists in man as a result of his separation from God.

King David provides clear evidence of his understanding of this fact. After David's great sin, when the prophet Nathan had come to prick his conscience, David knelt before God in a prayer of penitence. Now David had confessed to the prophet that his sin was worthy of death; yet, when David knelt before God in penitence and tears, this was his prayer, "Cast me not away from thy presence, and take not thy Holy Spirit from me" (Ps. 51:11). Why this prayer? Because David did not fear physical death, or more accurately, David feared something far more than physical death. He feared that he would be cast out from the presence of God.

Our Lord Himself spoke of the relative importance of these two, physical death on the one hand and spiritual death on the other. He said, "Fear not them who can destroy the body, but fear Him who is able to destroy both body and soul in hell." Fear not them who can destroy the body! Physical death is not that important. Passing out of the life of this world is not that important. To go or to stay is not that important. For this reason Stephen, being stoned, his body crushed and mangled, could look up with the light of glory upon his face. The world would say he was dying, but he was not. The life was about to be crushed from his body to be certain, but he was in closest fellowship with his God in that very hour. Tremble not, therefore, at the thought of physical death. Tremble, rather, at the thought of separation from the presence of God.

A two-fold tragedy lay in Adam's sin. Being separated from God, entering upon the state of spiritual death, his entire nature was corrupted. The branch which is separated from the vine withers and deteriorates. So Adam, being separated from the source of his life in God, found his spiritual nature withered and deteriorated. The image of God, in which he had been created, was now defiled. Once his mind had been capable of a right knowledge of God. Henceforth his knowledge of God would be perverted. Once his will was capable of conforming to the will of God. Henceforth he would be incapable of performing the will of God. Once his affections were pure. Henceforth his affections would be defiled and lustful.

Theologians refer to this condition as "total depravity." By total depravity, we mean, every area of man's nature is corrupt, so much so, that he is incapable of a right relationship to God. Both the Westminster Confession and the Heidelberg Catechism declare that man is "prone by nature to hate God and his neighbor" (Heidelberg, Q. 5). This condition is a result of man's separation from God. Man's incapacity for a right relationship to God results from his condition of spiritual death (Eph. 2:1).

Further, he would transmit this corrupted nature to his posterity, even to the present hour. Not one soul in the history of the race has escaped the corruption of Adam. Why? Because he is the father of us all. From Adam's loins we are sprung. From him we have received, not the image of God with which he was created but the corrupted, perverted image which resulted from spiritual death. This is why Job asked, "Who can bring a clean thing out of an unclean?" and answered, "Not one" (Job 14:4). This is why David wrote, "Behold, I was shapen in iniquity; and in sin did my mother conceive me" (Ps. 51:5). Again, this is why Paul wrote, ". . . There is none righteous, no not one. . . . There is none that seeketh after God . . . there is none that doeth good, no, not one" (Rom. 3:10-12). Why? Because each successive generation has inherited the corrupted nature of the preceding generation, back to Adam.

Further, out of the corruption of our natures springs all the evil deeds we commit. External temptations arise in the world to be sure, but the root of man's evil lies within his own breast, in the corrupted nature which is the hallmark of spiritual death. This is why man's condition is hopeless. Rather than satisfying the outraged justice of God, man sins the more daily, thereby adding to his indebtedness. How, then, shall man escape from the state of spiritual death into which he had plunged himself? Utterly incapable of helping himself, how shall man satisfy the demands of divine justice and become reconciled to God?

God provided the answer in the "Second Adam" (I Cor. 15:45-47). God did through his Son what man could never do for himself. God would send his Son into the world to undo all the damage the first Adam had done; thus, the apostle Paul refers to Him as the "Last Adam." Perhaps no passage is more pertinent at this point than Paul's word to the Galatian church, "When the fullness of time was come, God sent forth his Son, made of a woman, made under the law, To redeem them that were under the law, that we might receive the adoption of sons" (Gal. 4:4-5).

Note the particulars of Paul's declaration. The Second Adam would be "made of a woman." Why? That he might be true man, a member of the human race, like "unto his brethren in all things, sin excepted." Scarcely had the first sin of the race been committed when God gave the promise, the essence of the "covenant of grace," that the seed of the woman would bruise the serpent's head (Gen. 3:15). Now the seed of the woman was come. He would take his flesh and blood from the virgin Mary. As such, he would be true man, nothing more, nothing less, as to his human nature.

Secondly, we would be made "under the law." Does some-one ask, "What law?" In the final analysis, there is but one law, "Thou shalt love the Lord thy God with all thy heart, with all thy soul, with all thy mind, and with all thy strength." Even the second commandment is directly derived from the first, "Thou shalt love thy neighbor as thyself." Thus He would stand before the law, just as Adam had at the be-ginning. He must live in pure and perfect righteousness before God. The meditations of his heart and the words of his lips must be acceptable in the sight of God, even as must be the deeds of his hands.

Having accomplished all this, standing before God in per-fection and righteousness, He must bear the first Adam's pen-alty, that is, He must die. Now take care. Too many think of the death of Christ in the purely physical sense, the nails in his hands and feet, the ultimate departure of the soul from the body, and the body laid in the tomb. If this is all we see at Calvary, we shall have missed the heart of the atonement. We have already seen that the true nature of death is separa-tion from God. This is the experience He must endure upon the cross. He must be cut off from God. He must be forsaken of the Father. This is why we hear the cry, "My God, my God, why hast thou forsaken me?"

We must note quickly, too, the experience of Christ upon the cross went far beyond that of the first Adam in his exclu-sion from the garden. You see, man's separation from God is never final nor complete in this world. For as long as man remains in the world, he is never utterly cut off from God. The wicked are sustained by God's providence, even though they fail to acknowledge it. The rain falls upon the just and the unjust. God makes the sun to shine upon the wicked along with the righteous. In these, as well as in a multitude of other ways, all men are sustained by God's providence. They are not utterly cut off from his care.

The experience into which Christ entered at Calvary was that ultimate, complete, final separation from God. This is the third form of death of which Scripture speaks. We have noted that spiritual death consists in separation from God, but not in complete and final separation. When a man is completely cut off from God, so that only desolation and darkness remain — this is called "eternal death." And this is synonymous with hell. The two terms, "eternal death" and "hell," have an equivalent meaning in Scripture. This is why the Apostles' Creed refers to Christ's experience with the desolation and darkness in these words, "He descended into hell." When we hear Jesus cry, "My God, my God, why hast thou forsaken me?" we must realize this is a cry from the very depths of hell.

Why must Jesus enter upon the state of "eternal death," or again, why must He "descent into hell"? We have noted that this is the heart of the atonement. Precisely at this point He bore the ultimate penalty of Adam and of mankind. This we call the substitutionary atonement; that is, He took the place of the sinner and did what the sinner could never do for himself, to wit, He satisfied the justice of God.

Hear Isaiah's words, "Surely He hath borne our griefs and carried our sorrows ... he was wounded for our transgressions, he was bruised for our iniquities: the chastisement of our peace was [laid] upon him; and with his stripes we are healed. ... He was oppressed and he was afflicted, yet he opened not his mouth: he is brought as a lamb to the slaughter, and as a sheep before his shearers is dumb, so he opened not his mouth" (Isa. 53:4-7). Ah, but this is not all! The atonement was not yet complete! The prophet continued, "He was cut off out of the land of the living: for the transgression of my people was he stricken" (Isa. 53:8). And then He cried out! When he was cut off out of the land of the living, then He cried, "My God, my God, why hast thou forsaken me?" Then we know He is treading the winepress of the wrath of God alone. Then we know he is in the land of the dead, the eternally dead, where there is only darkness and desolation forever.

Then, and only then, could Paul declare, "For as in Adam all die, even so in Christ shall all be made alive" (I Cor. 15:22). At this moment the death penalty was fulfilled, not before. Now, in the darkness, He is enduring complete, utter, final separation from God. If He is to take the sinner's place, so that the sinner may live, He must enter upon "eternal death"; He must descend into the depths of hell. When, therefore, we hear the cry, "My God, my God, why hast thou forsaken me?" we know the price has been paid, the ultimate penalty has been exacted, the justice of God has been satisfied — not before.

Even so, men continue to ask, "But why this cry from the lips of Christ?" One basic answer may be given. Because He loved God still. In the darkness of desolation we see most clearly exhibited his perfect obedience to the Father. Made under the law, He must love God with all his heart, with all his soul, with all his mind, and with all his strength. How long must He love God so? Forever! He must love God in the agony of the garden. He must love God as the Roman lash is laid across his back. He must love God as the nails are driven into his hands and feet. Above all, He must love God in the very depths of the darkness. There, in the pit of hell, He must love God with all his heart, with all his soul, with all his mind, and with all his strength.

This is what gave birth to that wailing cry out of the darkness, "My God, my God, why hast thou forsaken me?" For sinful man, this would be no question. To be forsaken of God is the just penalty for sin. But why this One who loved God with a perfect love, who was obedient even unto death, yea the death of the cross — why should He be forsaken of the Father? To every child of God, we must say, there is but one answer: For you. For you, He suffered. For you, He died. For you, He went out into the darkness.

For you, He was "smitten of God and afflicted," even as the prophet had written eight centuries earlier. Nothing man could do to Him could bring forth that awful cry. Not what man did to Him, nor what demons did to Him wrought the cry, "My God, my God, why hast thou forsaken me?" This is what God did to Him for our redemption! This is why He must also be "very God of very God." Why? To bear the persecution of men? Others have borne persecution no less severe. To bear the onslaught of Satan? Others, by the grace of God, have stood. Why, then, must He be "very God of very God"? That He might sustain the infinite burden of the wrath of God by the infinite strength of his Godhead.

Hear again the word of Paul to the Galatians, "When the fullness of time was come, God sent forth his Son, made of a woman, made under the law, to redeem them that were under the law, that we might receive the adoption of sons" (Gal. 4:4-5). To redeem them that were under the law. That we might receive the adoption of sons.

See the Prodigal Son return from the far country of sin. In the providence and grace of God, he has learned the folly of life in the far country. Now he would return to his father's house. Hear him cry, "Father, I am no longer worthy to be called thy son." How true! Once God had a son in Eden. They walked and talked together in the garden in the cool of the day. The Father loved his son, but the son did not return his Father's love; rather, he rebelled against his Father and his God. Now Adam must also say, "Father, I am no longer worthy to be called thy son." Now the race of men must say, "Father, we are no longer worthy to be called thy children." Nonetheless, the father threw his arms about the prodigal, welcoming him back into the bosom of the family. Even so, our Father in heaven welcomes back into the bosom of the family those who have been "adopted of grace for Christ's sake."

This is why "Him who knew no sin was made to be sin on our behalf...." Why? "That we might become the righteousness of God in him" (II Cor. 5:21). This is why "He bore in his own body our sins," affixing the handwriting thereof to the tree of the cross. This is why He went out into the darkness, bearing the burden of our sin and guilt, that He might leave them out in the darkness forever, so that God should remember our sins no more.

Lest any should misunderstand, however, we must add a sobering thought. The atonement is not universal; it is not for all men. When Paul wrote, "As all die in Adam ...," he spoke of all men, the entire race. Why? Because all men were "in Adam." The entire race is sprung from Adam's loins.

When, however, Paul wrote, ". . . so shall all be made alive in Christ," he spoke, obviously, of those who are "in Christ." But all men are not in Christ! Some are "in Christ," but some are outside Christ. Therefore, some must enter upon eternal death for themselves. Some must go out into the darkness of desolation, even as He did!

Recall the scene in the Upper Room. Our Lord was about to institute the sacrament of his death and resurrection. Soon He must go to the garden. On the morrow He will go to the cross. First, however, He must point out the betrayer. When Judas departed the Upper Room, the Scriptures make this significant comment, "He . . . went immediately out, and it was night" (John 13:30). Yes, the shades of the physical night had fallen. The rays of the sun no longer bathed the earth. But the Scriptures mean so much more than this. The night into which Judas went out was the night of lost souls. Tomorrow Christ will go out into the darkness of desolation to atone for the sins of men, but Judas is not numbered among those for whom He went out into the darkness. Judas must go out into the darkness for himself. He went out, and it was night.

This is why we preach the gospel. This is why we continue to cry, "Repent, everyone of you and be baptized." We have seen the darkness. We have heard his cry, "My God, my God, why hast thou forsaken me?" And we know, unless He went out into the darkness in your behalf, you must go for yourself. Knowing the terror of the Lord, therefore, we persuade men: Be ye reconciled to God.

5. Hell's Aftermath: I Thirst

I thirst. — John 19:28

About six o'clock in the morning Pilate passed sentence upon Jesus, executing the order that He should be crucified. Almost three hours passed before the crucifixion took place. During this period Jesus struggled beneath the weight of the cross, bringing it at last to the place of death. At Calvary they drove the nails into his hands and feet, and the cross was mounted with Jesus upon it by nine o'clock. For three hours Christ hanged upon the cross, while the burning eastern sun intensified the agony of the crucifixion. At noon the light of the sun was extinguished, and a cloak of darkness was cast over the earth for a period of three hours. About three o'clock in the afternoon the darkness was dispelled as suddenly as it had appeared, and the light of the sun shone down upon the earth once more.

Nine hours had passed, therefore, since Jesus had been led forth from Pilate's judgment hall, nine hours of suffering, nine hours of pain, nine hours without a crust of bread or a drop of water to moisten his tongue. Then from the lips of Jesus came these words, "I thirst."

At first this simple statement may appear to be the most easily understood of all the words Christ uttered as He hanged upon the cross. Superficial observation might lead us to conclude that these words might have been spoken by any other man under comparable circumstances. As such, they appear to contrast sharply with the other "words" of Jesus from the cross.

When we hear the prayer of Christ, "Father, forgive them, for they know not what they do," our reaction is, no other man could have uttered these words. Another man might well have cursed those who brought about his death rather than offering prayer in their behalf. When we hear Him declare to the repentant thief, "Today, thou shalt be with me in paradise," we sense, intuitively, only the Eternal Son, Himself very God of very God, could have spoken these words. After all, none but God is competent to pronounce judgment upon the soul of man, admitting him into the heavenly kingdom. When we see Him look down from the cross upon Mary and John and hear Him say, "Woman, behold thy son. . . . Behold thy mother," we are amazed at this amazing Christ whose first consideration was for those whom He loved, even as He endured the excruciating agony of the cross. Again, when we hear Him cry, "My God, my God, why hast thou forsaken me?" we know only the sinless Savior could have uttered these words. Only one who was Himself without sin could question the rejection of God.

By contrast, the words, "I thirst," seem so thoroughly human, so simple, so uncomplicated, so self-evident in meaning. Certainly the theological liberal has no difficulty in interpreting these words. For the theological liberal, Jesus was simply a man dying an unfortunate death. Like any other man under similar circumstances He thirsted, and the reasons for his thirst were purely physical and natural. There are also many sincere but misguided evangelicals who find no difficulty in understanding these words. For some Jesus was the Son of God, to be certain, but He is nonetheless viewed as being helpless in his predicament at Calvary. They see Him shorn of all power, a helpless, pitiful, pathetic figure upon the cross.

Neither view does justice to the person and work of the God-man who wrought our redemption. Hear his words, "I lay down my life that I might take it again. No man taketh it from me, but I lay it down of myself. I have power to lay it down, and I have power to take it up again" (John 10:17-18). Know that only God could speak like this. This is precisely what poses the problem when we hear Him say, "I thirst." Why should He, the God-man, thirst — even upon a cross?

He is the one of whom John wrote, "All things were made by him, and without him was not anything made that hath been made" (John 1:3). Through Him God "...made the firmament, and divided the waters which were under the firmament from the waters which were above the firmament..." (Gen. 1:7). He is the one through whom "the waters under the heaven" were "gathered together unto one place," and the "dry land" was made to "appear" (Gen. 1:9-10). More, during his earthly ministry, He transformed the water into wine. He multiplied the five barley loaves and two small fishes, until the multitude was fed, and twelve baskets remained. Does it not seem strange that this kind of man, the God-man, should cry, "thirst" — even from a cross?

Paul supplies the answer in these words, "...He humbled himself, and became obedient unto death, even the death of the cross" (Phil. 2:8). When, therefore, we hear Him cry, "I thirst," we must realize, this cry was born out of his voluntary self-humiliation. The key to his cry lies in this: He humbled Himself! When we read, "I am poured out like water.... My strength is dried up...and my tongue cleaveth to my jaws; and thou hast brought me into the dust of death" (Ps. 22:14-15), we must know this is not, first of all, the work of man but the work of God. Of the Son we must say, "He humbled himself." Of the Father we must say, "Thou hast brought [Him] to the dust of death."

Be assured, there is no other reason, neither in heaven nor upon earth, that our Lord should have suffered the pangs of thirst even upon the cross, except that the redemptive purpose of God might be fulfilled. A mere word from his lips, a nod of his head would have brought the legions of the angels to minister to his needs. Recall his temptation in the wilderness. Forty days and forty nights Christ was without food in the wilderness of temptation. When Satan had departed, Matthew adds, "Behold, angels came and ministered to him" (Matt. 4:11). Forty days and forty nights the angels had waited in abeyance, listening for the call that would bring them to his side.

Nor was our Lord unaware of the proximity of the angels or of his lordship over the heavenly creatures. Hear Him say to Peter in the garden, "Thinkest thou that I cannot now pray the Father, and he shall presently give me more than twelve legions of angels?" In the same breath He added, "But how then shall the Scriptures be fulfilled, and thus it must be" (Matt. 26:53-54). So we ask, "Thinkest thou that he could not have prayed the Father, even from the cross, and the angels would have come on lightning wing to minister to his needs?" Why, then, should He cry out, "I thirst"? The reason remains the same, namely, that the Scriptures might be fulfilled. Thus John wrote, ". . . Jesus, knowing that all things were now accomplished, that the Scriptures might be fulfilled, saith, I thirst."

Secondly, John's word of explanation enables us to understand the circumstances which created the condition of thirst. What are the "all things" which had been "accomplished"? All things necessary to the redemption of his people. The larger context is surely his entire mediatorial work from his entry into the world to the very hour of his cry. The more immediate context is the atonement of the cross. Indeed, we shall not really understand the cry, "I thirst," until we realize it was born out of the experience through which he had just passed.

Two serious errors of interpretation are commonly made at this point. The first, for all practical purposes, isolates the cry, "I thirst," from the experience of Jesus which immediately preceded it upon the cross. Then the following interpretation is given. Prior to this point, Jesus had been engaged in a deep spiritual experience. The culmination was reached in his hour of desolation when He had been forsaken of the Father. Now the heart of the atonement had been completed. For the first time, therefore, he could think of his own needs. Thus, no heed is paid to the fact that his thirst was born out of the very experience through which He had just passed.

The second error is closely related. It is based upon the assumption that the cry, "I thirst," arose out of purely physical considerations. Even the late, great Abraham Kuyper wrote in the book, *His Decease at Jerusalem,* "As the Man of sorrows hanged on the cross to die, one complaint only was uttered about the suffering of his soul, and likewise only one complaint about suffering after the body. Utter anguish of soul forced from Him the (cry), 'My God, my God, why hast thou forsaken me?' and the agonizing death struggle after the flesh drew from Him the cry, 'I thirst.'" Thus, you see, the one word is assumed to result from a spiritual condition. The other is assumed to result from a physical condition.

We readily confess that both statements contain an element of undoubted truth. We must insist, however, that the two cannot be separated from each other, as though no relationship existed between them. The wrath of God, as it falls upon the whole man in body and soul, cannot be broken down into factors and forces, the one for the body, another for the soul. Neither can the nature of man be dissected and compartmentalized, the body here, the soul there.

Kuyper, unlike many who express similar views today, lived and wrote before the era of psychosomatic medicine. Strangely, or so it seems to us, only in recent years have medical practitioners paid serious heed to the inter-relationship of the spiritual, the mental, and the physical. Today, as never before, physicians recognize that many physical conditions result from spiritual-mental causes. Lay people are usually surprised to learn that within the memory of present day ministers of the gospel, the pastors of churches were not welcomed into the hospitals when they came to visit members of their congregations. Until recently the medical profession held that the patient's spiritual condition had no bearing upon illness or healing, and therefore, the pastor was believed to have no function at the patient's bedside.

Significantly, even the most recent works on the death of our Lord seem to ignore the spiritual-mental-physical inter-relationship in the nature of man. This we dare not do, if we are to comprehend the depth of meaning in the cry of Christ.

We must recognize the most intimate relationship between the spiritual experience through which He had just passed, the desolation and darkness which gave birth to the cry, "My God, my God, why hast thou forsaken me?" and his present physical condition described in the words, "I thirst."

We must do injustice neither to the physical nor the spiritual causes of the cry. Before we consider the spiritual factor in his condition, therefore, we should pay heed to the physical cause of his cry. Six hours He had hanged upon the cross. Once during this period He had been offered a drink commonly given to men under similar circumstances. Ancient writings indicate that it contained a narcotic property, intended to desensitize the body to pain in some measure. This He had refused. Neither his sensory perceptors nor his spiritual acuteness might be stultified. He must bear the full weight of the wrath of God in body, mind and soul.

Meantime, according to Christian physicians who have given study to the matter, the wounds in his body would, in all probability, have become infected. The infection would create a feverish condition. The fever, the abnormal body temperature, in turn, would produce dehydration. Again, modern medical science contributes to our understanding of the condition of Christ. Only in relatively recent years have doctors emphasized the factor of dehydration. They hasten to correct the condition by introducing a saline solution into the body.

We readily recognize these physical factors. We insist, however, that they are but one element, perhaps the lesser one, in giving birth to the cry, "I thirst." We dare not dismiss his prior experience, spiritual though it was, which gave birth to the cry, "My God, my God, why hast thou forsaken me?" What was the nature of this experience? The Apostles' Creed declares, "He descended into hell." Commenting upon this aspect of our confession, the catechism speaks of "his inexpressible anguish, pains, terrors, and hellish agonies in which He was plunged during all his suffering, but especially on the cross . . ." (Heidelberg, Q. 44).

Admittedly, many fail to realize that this is the meaning of the confession, "He descended into hell," his desolation, that He was forsaken by God while He hanged upon the cross. They assume, after his Spirit departed his body, and while the body was laid at rest in the tomb, He visited the abode of the unsaved dead, namely, hell. Bear in mind, therefore, his explicit statement to the repentant thief, "Today thou shalt be with me in paradise." Hear, too, his last word from the cross, "Father, into thy hands I commit my Spirit."

This should settle the matter once and forever. Perhaps, however, someone will remark, "But this or that passage seems to indicate otherwise." We must always bear in mind a foremost principle of Scriptural interpretation. Accept what is clear and explicit. Interpret all else, the figurative, the symbolic, and the unclear or doubtful in the light of what is explicit and clear. If we accept the word of Christ to the repentant thief at its face value, "Today thou shalt be with me in paradise," we shall not allow any other passage to disturb us. After all, Scripture is a unity. No passage of Scripture contradicts any other. If any other passage seems contradictory, the cause must lie in our own misinterpretation. The Bible does not contradict itself. Only our misconceptions contradict each other. Therefore, accept what is explicit and clear and know that nothing can contradict it.

If, however, the Spirit of Christ was committed into the hand of the Father at the time of physical death, if He along with the repentant malefactor was translated into paradise that very day, when, then, did He "descend into hell"? Upon the cross, in the darkness of desolation. This is, after all, the meaning of hell, to be utterly cut off from God. When we hear Him cry, "My God, my God, why hast thou forsaken me?" we must know that this cry arose from the very depths of hell.

You see, when God utterly withdraws, that is hell. Whenever and wherever God withdraws, that is hell. This does not imply that hell is something less than our forefathers in the faith proclaimed it to be. We do believe that all the unsaved dead are gathered together in a particular place. We do believe that following the judgment, all the unsaved of all ages shall again be gathered into a particular place. Hell is by no means a mere attitude or frame of mind. Nonetheless, hell is what it is, because it is the place where God is not. So when God withdrew while the Savior hanged upon the cross, forsaking his only begotten Son, Jesus was plunged into the depths of hell.

Everything we know concerning hell stems from this one basic fact, forsakenness by God. Hell is indeed the place where the scorpion is whose worm dieth not. Hell is indeed the lake which burneth with fire forever and ever. From hell comes the weeping, the wailing, the gnashing of teeth. There the unsaved shall bear the wrath of God forever, even as Jesus bore it upon the cross. And this is the epitome of the wrath of God, to be cast away from his presence, to be turned out into the night of desolation, to be utterly forsaken of God. Because God is not there, the scorpion is there whose worm dieth not. Because God has withdrawn, the lake burns with eternal fire.

When John writes, "After this, knowing all things were accomplished, that the Scripture might be fulfilled, He cried, I thrist," we must know that this is his reference. His atoning work was accomplished to be sure, and at the depth of it lay his ultimate experience with the wrath of God, to be forsaken of the Father. A more detailed revelation is given us in the twenty-second psalm. The opening verse foretells the cry, "My God, my God, why hast thou forsaken me?" (Ps. 22:1). The earlier portions of the psalm describe the circumstances surrounding the cross. "I am a worm, and no man," and so they treated Him, as though He were bereft of all human dignity. " . . . a reproach of men and despised of the people," and so He was, for He came unto his own, and his own received Him not. "All they that see me laugh me to scorn: they shoot out the lip, they shake the head saying, He trusted on the Lord that he would deliver him: let him deliver him, seeing he delighted in him" (Ps. 22:6-8). All this was done. All this was accomplished. All this He bore.

Then follows the depth of his experience with hell, "I am poured out like water, and all my bones are out of joint: my heart is like wax; it is melted in the midst of my bowels. My strength is dried up like a potsherd; and my tongue cleaveth to my jaws; and thou hast brought me into the dust of death" (Ps. 22:14-15). Now, do you know why He cried, "I thirst"? "My tongue cleaveth to my jaws; and thou hast brought me into the dust of death" — yea, eternal death, separation from God, desolation and darkness. This is why He cried, "I thirst." Even as the psalmist said, "My soul thirsteth for God, for the living God: when shall I come and appear before God?" (Ps. 42:2).

Recall, too, the parable of the "Rich Man and Lazarus." When the rich man died, Jesus said of him, "And in hell he lifted up his eyes, being in torments . . . . And he cried and said, Father Abraham, have mercy on me and send Lazarus, that he may dip the tip of his finger in water and cool my tongue, for I am in anguish in this flame" (Luke 16:23-24). This is why He was poured out like water. This is why his tongue cleaveth to his jaw. This is why He cried, "I thirst." He had passed through the flame. He had been cast out into the lake that burneth with fire forever and ever. The fever of the body? Yes. But the torment of the flame much more. Never make less of his cry, "I thirst." He had gone out into that dry and barren land where there is only the flame and the darkness of eternal night forever.

Why should the Son of God have borne the agonies of hell? Come for a moment. Stand beside the well with the Samaritan woman. She had come to the well to draw water, just as she had a thousand, ten thousand times before. Little did she realize the significance of this day in her life. Beside the well stood a Man. He said to her, "Give me to drink." This is the only other occasion recorded in the gospels when Jesus indicated a need for drink. We can only conclude, as always we must, that this is given for our instruction.

Hear Him then. Pointing to the water which she drew He said, "Whosoever drinketh of this water shall thirst again: But whosoever drinketh of the water that I shall give him shall never thirst; but the water that I shall give him shall be in him a well of water springing up into everlasting life" (John 4:13-14). Perhaps the woman little understood, but the water of which He spoke was the water of life eternal, living water, which He would purchase upon the cross by his death.

He thirsted upon the cross, so that the redeemed of the Lord should never thirst. He passed through the dry and barren land, so that the redeemed of the Lord should never be called upon to pass that way. He went out into the lake that burneth with fire forever and ever, so that the redeemed of the Lord need never go that way. He was forsaken of God, so that the Redeemed of the Lord need never be forsaken of God. The cry, "I thirst," was redemption's cry! This was the cry of Him who "bore in his own body our sin," the cry of Him who went out into the night of desolation where there is only the darkness and the flame forever.

Bear this in mind, too, beloved, this is also the cry of the unreconciled. This is the moan of the lost. This is the wail of the damned. In the lake of fire, the lost suffer in the flame of God's wrath forever and ever. This shall be their cry through the endless ages, "I thirst! I thirst!"

O, the wrath of God upon sin! There is reason that the sun should turn to darkness and the moon to blood. There is reason that the heavens should be shaken, and the stars should fall in the day of judgment. There is reason for men to cry for the rocks and the mountains to fall upon them and hide them from the judgment of Him who is seated upon the throne. Beyond lies the place which has been prepared for the devil and his angels and for all those who bear the mark of the beast and worship his image. Beyond lies the dread country where all those who have lived in rebellion against God shall dwell eternally. They shall have their wish and more: They shall be forsaken of God.

Beyond lies the lake which burneth with fire forever and ever. Hear the cry of all those who have sought the things which moth and rust can corrupt. Hear the cry of those who were taken up with the world, the flesh and the devil. This is their cry, "I thirst." Out of the awful darkness that overhangs the burning lake comes the cry of the damned, "I thirst!"

Would to God that men might thirst now! Would to God that men might thirst after the "living water" now, for this is the division among men. Some, by the grace of God, thirst after righteousness, and this is the promise, "They shall be filled." But some continue to thirst after unrighteousness. They shall be turned into the darkness that overlies the flaming lake. Out of the darkness, out of the burning lake shall come their cry through the endless ages, "I thirst! I thirst!" Hear, therefore, the blessed invitation, "And the Spirit and the Bride say, Come. And let him that heareth say, Come. And let him that is athirst come. And whosoever will, let him take the water of life freely" (Rev. 22:17).

Hear one last word. He who thirsts after righteousness is already born of God. This is precisely why he thirsts after righteousness. The "dead in trespasses and sin" do not thirst after the living water. The corpse does not cry out from his coffin, "I thirst." Therefore, if you thirst for the living water, if you thirst after righteousness, if you thirst after the living God, you are born anew.

Why must we declare this? Because a new doctrine has been added to the Christian faith by some. It reads something like this: Christ sacrificed Himself, so that I need sacrifice nothing. Christ suffered, so that I need deprive myself of nothing. Christ was obedient to the will of God so that I may be disobedient, or as they say it, "Christ fulfilled the law, so that I may disregard it." Christ kept the Sabbath Day holy, so that I may use it for my own pleasure. Christ put God first in his life, so that I can put God last in mine.

No, most of you do not phrase your thoughts in words like these, no more than you cry with Job's wife, "Curse God and die." But this is how you live. Hear me well, then, for this is surely the Word of God. Were you the children of God, were you born of God, you would bring forth fruits worthy of God. We may say it now, as surely as the prophets and the apostles said it long ago, "Thus saith the Lord: You will either thirst after righteousness now, you will either thirst after the living water now, or you will thirst forever." Out of the darkness, out of the burning lake will come your cry through all the endless ages, "I thirst! I thirst!" Come, then, thirst after right-eousness now, and ye shall be filled.

6. It Is Finished: Man's Redemption

It is finished. — *John 19:30*

Our understanding of the sixth "word" from the cross will depend upon three considerations. These are, first, when it was spoken; secondly, how it was spoken; and thirdly, the content of the declaration itself.

Note first, then, the place of the sixth word in the time sequence of events pertaining to the death of our Lord. For six hours Christ had hanged upon the cross. From nine o'clock in the morning until midday, the hot eastern sun had poured down its merciless rays upon Calvary. At high noon the strange darkness descended upon the earth, continuing for three hours, that is, until three o'clock in the afternoon. Then, as suddenly and as unexpectedly as it had fallen, the darkness was lifted.

The supreme passion of the cross had now ended. The weight of the wrath of God, which had pressed from the lips of Christ the agonizing cry, "My God, my God, why hast thou forsaken me?" had now been lifted. The excruciating torment of soul and body through which our Lord had passed brought forth the words, "I thirst." After He had been given vinegar to drink, He said, "It is finished."

Perhaps, even so, someone will ask, "But what was finished? His body was still impaled upon the cross. Death had not yet come. His very words attest that his Spirit had not yet departed his body. What, then, was finished?" We must answer, the essential work of the atonement was finished. He had borne the full fury of the wrath of God, even unto desolation and darkness. He had been "stricken, smitten of God and afflicted."

71

Now only physical death remained, and this, the departure of his Spirit from his body, would provide complete release from the suffering and pain He endured.

To place the sixth word, not only with reference to time but also with reference to progress and event, we must return momentarily to his fifth utterance from the cross, spoken only moments earlier. John wrote, "And Jesus, knowing that all things were now accomplished [to the end], that the Scriptures might be fulfilled, saith, I thirst" (John 19:28). Only after this, only after all things had been accomplished, only after the Scripture had been fulfilled, could Jesus announce, "It is finished."

Next, we must consider the manner in which the words were spoken. An age old truth holds that the manner in which one speaks may be more important than the words which are spoken. Words spoken calmly and quietly may have a quite different meaning than the same words when spoken harshly and angrily. The same words may speak of anger or peace, love or hate, hope or discouragement, sorrow or joy — it depends upon how they are spoken. In this instance, the words themselves hold vast import, but the manner in which our Lord uttered them is not insignificant. How, then, did Jesus speak the words, "It is finished"?

Note first, Jesus' voice contained no note of resignation or helplessness when He uttered these words. I have heard these words uttered in a tone of abject helplessness. A member of a congregation we formerly served suffered for many months in the terminal stage of a malignancy. At last God released her from the suffering of the body. When I arrived at the home shortly afterward, her daughter met me at the door. There were no tears in her eyes, but there was a hollow note in her voice when she said simply, "It's finished." The suffering was finished. The long days and nights of watching a mother die were finished. The tone of her voice added, however, "But I did not want it this way." She was a child of God, the daughter. She expressed no attitude of rebelliousness against the plan for her mother's life. This was the will of God, and she accepted it. Even so, one knew she would have spared her mother the suffering, had that been possible. One knew she longed for her mother's presence, but she had been helpless to avert either suffering or death. Thus the note of resignation, of helplessness when she said, "It's finished."

No such note was to be found in the Savior's voice when He said, "It is finished." The cross was not beyond his control. He was not helpless before the evil forces of men or demons. He went to the cross that all things might be accomplished, and therefore, that the Scripture might be fulfilled. At a decisive point in his ministry, Matthew records, "From that time forth began Jesus to show his disciples, how that he must go into Jerusalem, and suffer many things of the elders and chief priests and scribes, and be killed, and raised again the third day. Then," we read, "Peter took him, and began to rebuke him, saying, Be it far from thee, Lord: this shall not be unto thee. But [Jesus] turned and said unto Peter, Get thee behind me, Satan: thou art an offense unto me, for thou savorest not the things that be of God, but those that be of men" (Matt. 16:21-23).

Peter would have deterred Christ from the cross, because he "savored not the things of God," that is, he failed to comprehend redemption's plan. Jesus would go to the cross, because, in the going, man would be reconciled to God. Luke records that eight days later the "transfiguration" took place. Moses and Elijah appeared with Christ on the "Mount of Transfiguration" and "spake of his decease which *he* should accomplish at Jerusalem" (Luke 9:31). Soon after, we read, " . . . when the time was come that he should be received up, he steadfastly set his face to go to Jerusalem" (Luke 9:51).

So He arrived at Jerusalem. So He was crucified, but we cannot believe that He was helpless, even upon the cross. We recall once again his words, "I lay down my life that I may take it again. No man taketh it from me. I lay it down of myself." He was nailed to the cross, because, and only because, He chose to be nailed to that cross. He remained upon the cross, only because He willed to remain upon it. Not for a moment was He helpless, either before those who condemned Him or before those who crucified Him. Only of Him may it truly be said, "He was the Master of his fate! He was the captain of his soul!"

When, therefore, we hear Him say, "It is finished," we detect no note of helplessness. To the contrary, these were words of satisfaction. What was finished? The work He had set out to do was finished! Men and demons had thought to finish Him at the cross. Instead, He had used them to the accomplishment of his own purpose. To this end He had come into the world. Now the task was completed; the work was done; the atonement was accomplished. Therefore He could say, not in resignation but with satisfaction, "It is finished."

These were words of satisfaction, expressed toward a task well done. An equivalent may be found in the creation account of Genesis. At the conclusion of God's creative activity one may read, "Thus the heavens and the earth were *finished*, and all the host of them" and, for that matter, all things contained therein (Gen. 2:1). The depth of meaning in the verb "finished" comes to us only as we read the account of the six creation days. On the first day God created the heavens and the earth and divided the light from the darkness. Then we read, "And God saw . . . that it was good" (Gen. 1:4). On the second day God created the firmament, divided the waters and caused the dry land to appear. Again we read, " . . . and God saw that it was good" (Gen. 1:10). On the third day God caused the earth to bring forth grass, herbs and trees. And again, " . . . God saw that it was good" (Gen. 1:12). On the fourth day God created the celestial bodies, the sun, moon and stars. Again we read, " . . . and God saw that it was good" (Gen. 1:18). So at the close of each creation day, God looked upon what He had accomplished that day, and He saw that it was good. This is the fact we must bear in mind as we read, at the end of the sixth day, "Thus the heavens and the earth were *finished* . . . ." The creation was finished, and it was good.

Our word "good" bears a lesser connotation. God's creative work was more than "good." It was perfect, complete. He could look upon it with the satisfaction of a task well done. Recall, too, the Son was the "Mediator of creation." John wrote, "All things were made by him, and without him was not anything made that was made" (John 1:3). Through Him, God had wrought a perfect creation. Now, through Him, God wrought a perfect redemption. Even as God, through the Son, brought the creation into being, so after the creation was cursed by sin, God was in Christ reconciling the world unto Himself. When we hear Christ say, "It is finished," we must know that, even as God looked upon the creative work He had accomplished through the Son and saw that it was good, so now God could look upon the redemptive work He had accomplished through the Son and see that it was good — more than good, perfect and complete — finished!

So Christ spoke the words, "It is finished," with all the satisfaction of a great work well done. Those who heard Him were amazed. They understood so little. What was finished? They saw only a man nailed to a cross. He was still impaled upon the cross. The nails were still in his hands and feet. The wounds of the crown of thorns were still visible upon his brow. The stain of blood lay upon the wounds of the lash in his back. What, then, was finished? Wherein lay his satisfaction, his triumph, his victory? They saw only what men had done to Christ. They failed to see what God was doing, through Christ, for the world.

We have already indicated, the atonement was complete; yet, we shall not comprehend the length and breadth and depth of his accomplishment upon the cross, unless we see the atonement set in the larger context of the plan of God for the redemption of the world. This is the failure of many, as they seek to treat the sixth word from the cross. One remarks, "His suffering was finished." A second, "His experience with hell was finished." A third, "The atonement was finished." True, all true; yet, none of these statements do justice to the scope of the divine accomplishment at Calvary. The atonement may be likened to a gem set in a broach. The gem itself is magnificent, but its beauty is enhanced by the setting in which it is placed. Thus we must see the atonement as part of a larger plan, the plan of God for the redemption of the world.

The apostle Peter pointed in this direction with his declaration that Jesus was "delivered up by the determinate counsel and foreknowledge of God" (Acts 2:23). Zechariah refers to the same fact in terms of the "Counsel of Peace," saying, ". . . the counsel of peace shall be between them both" (Zech 6:13), that is, between the Father and the Son. The psalms provide further detail, for we read, "I will declare the decree: The Lord hath said unto me, Thou art my Son; this day have I begotten thee. Ask of me, and I shall give thee the heathen for thine inheritance, and the uttermost parts of the earth for thy possession" (Ps. 2:7-8).

From these and related passages we obtain the concept known as the "Covenant of Redemption." Perhaps we should spend a moment with the terminology. Man can scarcely grasp the basic spiritual nature of the "covenant" concept as it is set forth in Scripture. To us, a covenant is a contract. And a contract is a legal document. Further, a contract may become an instrument of coercion. Men may be compelled to act against their will or beyond their ability or suffer the consequences set forth in the contract. Such is far removed from the nature of the "covenant" between the Father and the Son. These two, loving each other with a perfect and eternal love, willingly, voluntarily and gladly enter into compact with each other for the redemption of men.

What was the nature of the covenant between the Father and the Son, the Covenant of Redemption? Simply not, perhaps too simply, in return for the sinless life and atoning death of the Son, the Father would present Him with an elect people, ordained unto eternal life through the shedding of his blood.

Thus, in a very real sense, the cross of Christ was erected first, not at Calvary but in the Counsel of Peace. In the "determinate counsel" of God, the Son was first impaled upon a cross. Thus John speaks in Revelation of ". . . the Lamb slain from the foundation of the world" (Rev. 13:8). Thus, too Peter wrote, ". . . ye were not redeemed with corruptible things, as silver and gold . . . but with the precious blood of Christ, as of a Lamb without blemish and without spot: Who verily was foreordained before the foundation of the world, but was manifest in these last times for you" (I Peter 1:18-20).

Still, as Peter pointed out, that which had been foreordained before the foundation of the world remained to be worked out in history. The Father and the Son entered into covenant before the foundation of the world. With the creation of man came the fall of man into sin. Centuries would pass before the Son would enter the human race as the God-Man, Jesus Christ. Then Paul wrote, "This is a faithful saying, and worthy of all acceptation, that Christ Jesus came into the world to save sinners..." (I Tim. 1:15). This was his work. This was his task. He must save sinners from the outraged justice of a holy God. He must redeem unto God a people, out of every tongue and tribe and nation, by the shedding of his precious blood.

Because all things had been determined before the worlds were framed, Jesus could outline for his disciples the events which lay ahead, even as Matthew wrote, "From that time forth began Jesus to show his disciples, how that he must go to Jerusalem, and suffer many things of the elders and chief priests and scribes, and be killed, and be raised again on the third day" (Matt. 16:21). This, too, is why Moses and Elijah could speak with Him beforehand of "his decease which he should accomplish at Jerusalem" (Luke 9:31). And this is why "... he set his face steadfastly to go to Jerusalem" (Luke 9:51).

He had covenanted with the Father for the redemption of men. To this end He had come into the world. The cross was ever before Him. Nothing must restrain Him or detain Him from the cross. Each step of the way, He walked according to the time-table which was formulated in the Counsel of Peace. At last the end was at hand. Men did not know, but He knew. On the first day of the week when He should die, He entered into Jerusalem. We call this event the "Triumphal Entry." The multitudes shouted, "Hosanna to the Son of David. Blessed is he that cometh in the name of the Lord" (Matt. 21:9). Earlier He had commanded his disciples "that they should tell no man that he was Jesus the Christ" (Matt. 16:20). Why, now, did He invite the plaudits of the multitude? Because the time was at hand. This was calculated to arouse the antagonism of the rulers of the Jews. Earlier He had avoided antagonizing them unnecessarily. They must not seek to bring about his death prematurely. But now that the time is at hand, He will arouse their anger and incur their wrath.

The same day "... Jesus entered ... into the temple, and ... looked round about upon all things" (Mark 11:11). He was planning the next day, even as it had been planned from eternity. He departed the city but returned on the morrow. Then He entered the courts of the temple, overthrew the tables of the money changers and drove out the sellers of doves. Why? Because the temple was being defiled? Yes, but much more; this was an act, above all others, calculated to fire the antagonism of the Jewish rulers to fever pitch.

The "temple cleansing" occurred on Monday. On Tuesday Jesus returned to the temple. Standing in the very court of the temple, He entered into open controversy with the rulers of the Jews. It was at this time that the Sadducees raised the question of the resurrection, presenting a case of a widow who married seven brothers successively. They asked whose wife she would be in the life hereafter. Jesus replied that after the resurrection, there would be neither marriage nor giving in marriage (Mark 12:25). It was at this time that the Pharisees and the Herodians came with their question, "Is it lawful to pay tribute to Caesar?" To which Jesus replied, "Render unto Caesar the things that are Caesar's, and unto God the things that are God's" (Mark 12:17).

Jesus' very ability to confound them incensed them the more. This was his purpose. Let them be angry now. Let them seek to take his life. Their hate would become an instrument of God to bring about the sacrifice of his Son. That night, we read, "The chief priests and the scribes sought how they might take him with craft and put him to death. *But* they said, *Not* on the feast day lest there be an uproar of the people" (Mark 14:1-2).

Meantime, the same evening, while the rulers of the Jews plotted against Him, Jesus said to his disciples, "Ye know that after two days is the feast of the passover, and the Son of man is betrayed to be crucified" (Matt. 26:2). The rulers of the Jews said, "Not on the passover." Jesus said, "On the passover," and on the passover He was crucified! Man did not determine the time of his death, any more than man determined the fact of it. Our Lord set the time, even as it had been predetermined from before the foundation of the world.

On Thursday night we hear Him pray, "Father, the hour is come ..." (John 17:1). Then we hear Christ continue, "I have glorified thee on the earth: I have finished the work thou gavest me to do" (17:4). What, specifically, had He done? One, "I have manifested thy name to the men which thou gavest me out of the world," and He added, "Thine they were, and thou gavest them me" (17:6). Two, "I have given unto them the words which thou gavest me; and they have received them ... and they have believed that thou didst send me" (17:8). Three, now He prays for them saying, "I pray for them, I pray not for the world, but for them which thou hast given me" (17:9). Four, "While I was with them in the world, I kept them in thy name; those that thou gavest me I have kept, and none of them is lost, but the Son of perdition; that the Scripture might be fulfilled" (17:12). On the morrow He would die for them. And when He had borne the wrath of God in their stead, He could say, "It is finished."

Consider, now, more exactly, the point at which He could say, "It is finished." It was not finished when they had driven the nails into his hands and feet. It was not finished when they planted the cross on Calvary's Hill. It was not finished when the crowd mocked and jeered. Indeed, nothing man could do to Him would expend the wrath of God upon sin. He must be stricken, smitten of God and afflicted. He must be cast into the outer darkness of desolation. Only after He had uttered that fearful cry, "My God, my God, why hast thou forsaken me?", only after God had worked on Him the infinite terror of desolation, was it finished.

When at last the darkness was dispelled, when at last the light of the sun shone down upon the earth once more, men could know that the plan of God, contemplated in the Counsel of Peace before the worlds were framed, had been brought to fruition and fulfillment in the world of men. When it was done, all done, He cried out triumphantly, "It is finished."

What was finished? His work under the Covenant of Redemption was finished. Yes, his suffering was finished. Yes, his awful experience with the desolation of hell was finished. He had drained the cup of God's wrath to the last bitter dreg. When all this and much more is summed up, the total of it is this: His work under the Covenant of Redemption was finished. He had done all He had covenanted to do before the worlds were framed. His work was perfect and complete. It was finished.

Additionally, we should note, never was there any question but that He would finish the work He had set out to do. Some make this conjecture, you know. One school of thought suggests that the Old Testament saints looked on with bated breath to see whether He would conquer the cross or be conquered by it. Ridiculous! God was in Christ working the redemption of men. To hint at the possibility of failure is to dishonor the Almighty. When will men cease to impute human frailty to God? What was foreordained from eternity most certainly must come to pass in time. Inexorably, inevitably, without possibility either of failure or delay, He would accomplish the task set before Him. When He had done just that, accomplished all that He had set out to do, He said, "It is finished."

Indeed, we may say in all truth, man's redemption was finished. Perhaps someone will suggest, "This is not quite true. The work of Christ was finished, but the redemption of man remains to be accomplished in their lives day by day." This is true, but we must realize that this, too, was settled upon the cross. It was settled, first, in the counsel of peace before the worlds were framed. It was settled in human history at Calvary. We can be assured of this fact, because the Father is no less faithful to his covenant than is the Son. Even as Jesus would not be detained nor restrained from the cross, so the Father will not be detained nor restrained from bringing men to redemption through his Holy Spirit.

Few men would undertake to dispute that God is sovereign, but many in their preaching would impute this attribute only to the Father. Many who profess the name of the Son nonetheless preach a whining, begging, pleading, helpless, powerless Savior. Even larger numbers preach a Holy Spirit who makes Himself available to all men, but who is helpless to move any apart from their willingness to be moved. Meantime they preach the corruption of human nature, apparently oblivious to their own illogic. For if man be truly "dead in trespasses and sins," he remains such, until the Holy Spirit executes a work of grace in his heart. The Holy Spirit can be nothing less than sovereign, if any man is to be saved. Only after the Holy Spirit has rendered the "heart of stone" into a "heart of flesh" can man respond to the overtures of divine mercy. The Father sends forth the Holy Spirit to work this transformation in the hearts of all those of whom Christ said, "Thine they were, and thou gavest them me" (John 17:6). Thus every soul for whom Christ died shall be found in the Church of the First Born, the Assembly of the Elect, in that last day. This the Father covenanted to do when the Father and the Son entered into the Covenant of Redemption.

Can we be sure? Jesus said, "All that the Father giveth me shall come to me, and him that cometh to me, I will in no wise cast out" (John 6:37). How often these words from the lips of Jesus are quoted, but only in part, " . . . him that cometh to me, I will in no wise cast out." Apparently many do not realize this is only the latter portion of the verse. Hear it carefully, then, "*All* that the Father giveth me *shall come* unto me," and indeed, "him that cometh to me, I will in no wise cast out." Why not? Because Father and Son have entered into covenant together for the redemption of a people. By the death of Christ, they have become his purchased possession. Therefore, the Father will bring them to Him one by one, calling them out of every tongue and tribe and nation and people. And He will not cast them out. Of course not! They were given to Him by the Father from eternity. For them He prayed. For them He died. Therefore, when the Father brings them to Him, He will not cast them out.

How will God fulfill his covenant with the Son? Jesus said, "No man can come unto me, except the Father who hath sent me draw him," and these the Father will draw unto Him. Again He said, "It is the Spirit that quickeneth [giveth life] ... no man can come unto me, except it were given him of my Father" (John 6:63-65). Though they be dead in trespasses and sin, the Father will quicken them. They will be born anew, " ... not of blood, nor of the will of the flesh, nor of the will of man, but of God" (John 1:13). Thus all who were given Him shall come to Him, and thus we read, "he shall see of the travail of his soul, and shall be satisfied ... " (Isa. 53:11).

Nor must we ever make the latter text to mean less than the Scripture intends. To many this means nothing more than that, when Christ sees those who have "accepted him," to use a common terminology, He will be satisfied; he will judge that his death was not in vain. Ah, but it means so much more than that. Because He knows, "All that the Father giveth me shall come unto me," He knows that every soul for whom his blood was shed shall be numbered among the redeemed in that last day. This is why "He shall see of the travail of his soul and shall be satisfied." Thus, when He said, "It is finished," He might have said just as correctly, "Their salvation is finished, The salvation of those whom thou hast given me is finished."

Now you must examine your own heart to determine whether your salvation was finished at Calvary. How can you know? Hear Jesus say, "And this is the Father's will, who hath sent me, that of all whom he hath given me I should lose nothing, but should raise it up again at the last day" (John 6:39). In the following verse He added, "And this is the will of him that sent me, that everyone who seeth the Son, and believeth on him, may have everlasting life, and I will raise him up at the last day" (John 6:40). These two, those who have been given Him of the Father and those who believe upon Him in the world, are one and the same. Of them, He shall lose nothing, and He will raise them up at the last day. How, then, can one know whether he has been given to Christ from eternity? All those who possess a true and saving faith may know their faith is the gift of God. Because they have been given to Christ from eternity, God has created faith in their hearts.

This gives rise to a second question. How can one know whether He has a true and saving faith in Christ, and therefore, whether his salvation was finished on the cross? Hear the words of John, "And hereby do we know that we know him, if we keep his commandments. He that saith, I know him, but keepeth not the commandments, is a liar, and the truth is not in him" (I John 2:3-4). Strong words these, but they speak to a fundamental fact of the spiritual life. You see, a true and saving faith is neither vague, indefinable nor nebulous. The marks of a true and saving faith may be seen daily in the lives of those who truly belong to Christ. They keep his commandments. This is why He Himself said, "If ye love me, keep my commandments" (John 14:15).

Some appear to make a deliberate effort to complicate the Christian Faith. They ask, "How can I know, if I am truly a child of God? How can I know whether I am one of those for whom Christ died at Calvary? How can I know whether I am numbered with the elect who were given to Him by the Father in the Counsel of Peace before the worlds were framed?" You can know! The Word of God tells you how you can know, "Hereby do we know that we know him, if we keep his commandments. He that saith, I know him, but keepeth not the commandments, is a liar, and the truth is not in him."

Perhaps someone is saying in his heart, "But I have not known Christ in this way. I have not kept the commandments." For you, we have another question, "Do you want to know Him? Do you want to do the will of God? Do you want to be at peace with God?" If you have this desire, the grace of God is at work in you. Stand beside the Philippian Jailer as he asks his great question, "What must I do to be saved?" Hear the answer of Paul, "Believe on the Lord Jesus Christ, and thou shalt be saved, and thy house." From the moment that you are able to say, from a faith born of God in your heart, I know that Christ died for me — from that moment you will also know that you were given to Him from eternity.

7. Peace at the End

Father, into thy hands I commend my spirit. — Luke 23:46

Nowhere is the Lordship of Christ over his passion more clearly revealed than in his last "word" from the cross. Note closely Luke's record, "And when Jesus had cried with a loud voice, He said, Father, into thy hands I commend my Spirit." Since none of us has witnessed death by crucifixion, we are not immediately struck by the incongruity of the comment that He cried with a "loud voice." For a crucified man to cry with a loud voice after six hours upon the cross is, humanly speaking, impossible.

Have you ever questioned the specific cause of death in the instance of crucifixion? The nails in the crucified one's hands and feet were excruciatingly painful but clearly not the cause of death. And the body usually was not afflicted in any other way. What, then, produced death? The answer must be: paralysis of the respiratory system. The weight of the body on the muscular structure of the respiratory system produced a paralysis of the system. Soon the crucified one's breathing became labored and heavy. Each breath became increasingly difficult and painful, until at last the respiratory system functioned no more.

This is why the legs of the two malefactors were broken to hasten death. When each breath became an agony for the crucified one, he would push downward on the nails which pinned his feet, relieving the respiratory system of the weight of the body. Thus he would breathe more easily for a few moments. Once his legs were broken, however, he could no longer relieve his labored breathing. When at last complete paralysis set in, the respiratory system failed to function and death occurred.

We should not indulge in these tasteless details, were they not essential to understanding our Lord's death. No man could have cried with a loud voice after six hours on the cross. The cry of our Lord, therefore, is a further testimony to his Godhead. His forceful cry should be immediately related to his words, "No man taketh my life. I lay it down of myself." Even on the cross, He was in complete command of the situation. His death was not involuntary. To the contrary, when the atoning work of the cross was completed, He voluntarily and by an act of his own will released his Spirit from his body.

Having considered the extraordinary, unique character of our Lord's death, namely, that He could and did determine the time of his Spirit's departure from the body, we will also do well to consider certain parallels between his death and that of all other men. When we stand at the foot of the cross and hear the words of Christ, "Father, into thy hands I commend my Spirit," we must realize that we are standing in the presence of death, physical death. In this sense, the purely physical, the death of Christ was not different from that of other men.

Perhaps you will question this statement for a moment. You are thinking of the manner of his death, the crucifixion, the agony of the cross. You are thinking of the scene at Calvary, the jeering, decisive comments of the unthinking crowd milling about at the foot of the cross. You are thinking, too, of the spiritual aspect of his death, that He bore in his own body our sin, that He who knew no sin was made to be the Sin-Bearer, that we might become the righteousness of God through Him.

We do well to think on these aspects of his death, but we shall dismiss them for a moment — and only for a moment. For a moment we shall disregard both the historical setting and the deep spiritual implications of the death of our Lord to note that, whether a man die on a cross or in a modern hospital, whether a man be struck down by an automobile or by disease, the essential fact of physical death is the same for all.

Then we may gain insight into the real nature of physical death from the last word from the lips of Christ, "Father, into thy hands I commend my Spirit." This is the essential nature of physical death, the separation of soul and body, the departure of the soul or spirit from the body. Along with the words of Christ, we should hear the writer of Ecclesiastes, "Then shall the dust return to the earth as it was, and the spirit shall return to God who gave it" (12:7). Paul adds, ". . . If our earthly house of this tabernacle be dissolved, we have a building of God, a house not made with hands, eternal in the heavens" (II Cor. 5:1). The human body is, therefore, to be regarded as a dwelling, a place of residence. True, it is subject to decay and dissolution, but the man who resides therein simply moves on to another dwelling, a house not made with hands, eternal in the heavens.

Admittedly, the medical profession has another definition of death, a biological definition. For them, I suppose, a proper definition of physical "death" would be "the cessation of heart action." With this definition we have no argument. We merely note that this is a biological definition. It speaks of an observable, physical fact. The heart ceases to pulsate. As Christians we are aware, however, that physical death has a deeper meaning. Under the physical fact lies a spiritual fact, namely, the life principal, the spirit, the soul, the essential person has departed the body. The biological fact, that the body has ceased its organic function, is secondary. The spiritual fact, that the soul has departed the body, is primary.

We gain further insight into the true nature of the spiritual aspect of death from an earlier word from the cross, the "second word," spoken to the Repentant Malefactor. This man turned to Jesus in contrition and faith saying, "Jesus, Lord, remember me when thou comest into thy kingdom." Jesus replied, "Today thou shalt be with me in Paradise." This statement places two facts before us. First, it answers the question once and forever: Where did Christ, that is, the soul of the God-man, go immediately following the departure of his Spirit from his body? He entered into Paradise, that is, into the presence of God.

Further, the statement to the dying malefactor tells us more than the destination of Christ. We learn that what was true for our Savior is true for all of the children of God. Even as He would go into the blessed presence of the Father, so would the Repentant Malefactor. They would be together in Paradise. This is the assurance in which we rest our souls. If we have known Him in life, we shall likewise know Him in death. "Yea, though I walk through the valley of the shadow of death, I will fear no evil, for thou art with me . . ." (Ps. 23:4). "Today, thou shalt be with me in Paradise."

Secondly, we note the words of Jesus as the last words of a dying man. Many people place considerable weight upon the last words of a dying man. Perhaps this was more common a generation ago than it is today; yet, some continue to ask the loved ones of the departed, "Did you have a last word?" The implication is that one cannot be completely certain of the salvation of the departed one, unless he has spoken a final word of reassurance concerning the state of his soul.

An excellent Christian woman came to the study one day with real concern upon her heart. Her husband had passed away a few weeks before. She had been secure in her knowledge that he was a child of God. His entire life had been a testimony to the faith in his heart. Then a neighbor visited the widow. She had remarked, "I would not want to see my husband die without speaking a word of reassurance concerning his salvation."

This set the widow to thinking. She knew her husband had lived a devout life, but now the question arose in her mind, "Should he have spoken some last word of reassurance, if he were truly a child of God? She need not have been concerned. Her husband was not to be compared with the Repentant Thief. Her husband had not lived in rebellion against God. To the contrary, her husband had acknowledged Christ as his Savior and Lord as a young man, and his life had been a testimony that his faith was real and true.

This, in the final analysis, is the important consideration, not what we say, but what we are, and therefore, what we do. The Scriptures declare, "We must all appear before the judgment seat of Christ, that every one may receive the things done in his body, according to that he hath done, whether it be good or evil" (II Cor. 5:10). In that last day, his devout and worshipful life will be the testimony to the faith which was in his heart through the years. He will have no need to plead, "Lord, Lord...." His life will testify to the true and saving faith which was in his heart.

Occasionally, someone does speak a fine word of faith in the last hours of his life. One beautiful statement came from the lips of a dying mother who said to her family, "I am walking with God today." This was in the morning. Before the evening shadows fell she had, indeed, walked with God — out of this world and into the next, her hand clasped in the hand of the Savior. Her family was deeply moved by this last word. So was I as her pastor, but I would have been no less certain of her salvation, had she spoken no word at all. Her entire life was a testimony to the reality of her faith. Those who knew her best needed no last word to convince them that she was a child of God. When she spoke, her words were but a confirmation of the faith which had been clearly evident in her life throughout the years.

Thirdly, we should observe a similar fact in the life of the dying Savior. His last word was a testimony to his entire earthly life. This is precisely what makes his last word meaningful. If, at the point of death, Pilate had uttered these words, "Father, into thy hands I commend my spirit," we would reply, "What you are, Pilate, speaks so loudly we cannot hear what you say. Your cowardice and political expediency in sentencing an innocent man to the cross make us doubt these last words you speak. Is it possible that you have experienced an 'eleventh hour' conversion?" Had Judas, the betrayer, spoken the words, "Father, into thy hands I commend my spirit," we would reply, "What you are, Judas Iscariot, speaks so loudly we cannot hear what you say. We hear, rather, the jingle of the thirty pieces of silver you took for betraying your Lord. We see, rather, the kiss of death which you planted upon his brow. No, Judas, we cannot hear your words."

When, however, we hear Jesus say, "Father, into thy hands I commend my Spirit," the words ring true. His entire life upon earth had been a testimony to his submission to the will of the Father. He had trusted the Father in life; therefore, He could trust the Father in death; and therefore, He could speak the words, "Father, into thy hands I commend my Spirit."

Fourthly, consider that this was, not only the last word of Christ from the cross but the seventh word. In this instance the number "seven" holds significance for us. Perhaps we should add that we have no intention of dabbling in the numerology of Scripture, nor would we wish to be categorized with those who profess such knowledge. This is presumptuousness. They are neither exegetes or expositors but speculators. Even so, we may know the number "seven" holds significance throughout Scripture. Everywhere in Scripture the number "seven" implies completion and fulfillment. With this principle before us we may note, as does the author of Hebrews, the parallels between the creative work of the Father and the redemptive work of the Son (Heb. 4:1-10). In six days God created the heavens and the earth, and all that in them is. At the close of the sixth day, the creative work was completed, and God declared that it was good. On the seventh day God rested.

In the rest of the seventh day we must find something quite different than the recuperation of strength in one who is worn and tired. To suggest that God rested because He was weary is to impute human weakness and frailty to God. After all, God is the omnipotent One. He called the worlds into being by the might of his power. He spoke, and it was done. Weariness is unknown to God. He has no need of rest in this sense. Since this is true, however, we must ask what the rest of the seventh day did mean to God. We reply that it meant completion, fulfillment, satisfaction. The great work of creation was completed. The architectural plan of God, if so we may term it, was brought to fruition and fulfillment in the completion of his creative work. And the work being completed, the task being done, and done perfectly, the rest of the seventh day was a rest of satisfaction, satisfaction in a task well done.

So with Jesus upon the cross. With the sixth word, "It is finished," He announced the completion of his redemptive work and the perfection of it. Note that we have said, not merely the completion of his work, but the perfection of it. It could not be complete, until it was perfect. His work was not done, until He had made the one perfect sacrifice forever for the sins of men. Therefore, when we hear Him say, "It is finished," we know, not merely that the work of redemption is done, but that it has been done perfectly. Even as the Father looks upon the creation and saw that it was "good," so the Son looked upon the work of redemption and saw that it was "good." Thus, with the seventh word, He could announce his contentment and assurance in the care of the Father.

When we say that the work of redemption, performed by our Savior upon the cross, was perfect and complete, what do we mean? At least two things. First, man can add nothing to the finished work of Christ. The writer to the Hebrews declares, " . . . we are sanctified through the offering of the body of Jesus Christ once for all" (Heb. 10:10) . Bear in mind, the root meaning of the verb "to sanctify" is "to cleanse." We are cleansed, therefore — not partially cleansed but completely cleansed of all sin and guilt — by the offering of the body of Jesus Christ once for all.

In the same chapter we are told the folly of seeking to make any other sacrifice for sin, "And every priest standeth daily ministering and offering oftentimes the same sacrifice for sin, which can never take away sins" (Heb. 10:11) . Hence the folly of the "bloodless sacrifice" of the Mass which Rome declares to be essential to salvation. Protestants refuse to dishonor the death of their Lord by suggesting any other sacrifice is either necessary or helpful. By grace through faith we know that our Lord offered his body "once for all."

Historic Protestantism does not, however, move to the other extreme which, for all practical purposes, relieves the professing Christian of all responsibility and obligation toward his God. We do not assume the simple statement, "I believe," is meaningful apart from a dedicated life. We take seriously the words of the same chapter, "Let us hold fast the profession of our faith without wavering.... And let us consider one another to provoke unto love and to good works: Not forsaking the assembling of ourselves together, as the manner of some is, but exhorting one another.... For if we sin wilfully after that we have received the knowledge of the truth, there remaineth no more a sacrifice for sins, but a certain expectation of the judgment..." (Heb. 10:23-27).

This, presumably, we all understand. There is, however, another kind of "works" by which men seek to add something to the sacrifice of Christ. This conception makes both repentance and faith to be the "works" of man. Now, let us have no misunderstanding. Must we repent of our sins? Of course we must. Must we believe on Christ as our Savior? Of course we must. But repentance and faith are the works of God in man, purchased for his people by Christ upon the cross. Thus the prophet wrote, "... turn thou me, and I shall be turned; for thou art the Lord my God" (Jer. 31:18). And again, "Turn thou us unto thee, O Lord, and we shall be turned..." (Lam. 5:21). That is, convert us, O Lord, and we shall be converted indeed.

Apparently this fact was clearly understood in the Apostolic church. After Peter had brought the gospel to Cornelius, often called the first Gentile convert, He was criticized by Jewish converts precisely because Cornelius was a Gentile. Peter, in turn, explained how the Holy Spirit had come upon Cornelius and his household. Then, we read, the critics "glorified God, saying, Then hath God also to the Gentiles granted repentance unto life" (Acts 11:18).

To sum up the matter, we must realize that by his finished work, Christ purchased for his people the unction of the Holy Spirit. All mankind, by nature, is dead in trespasses and sins (Eph. 2:1). Men are reborn, that is, made alive by the will of God (John 1:13; Rom. 9:16). The man who is made alive by the Holy Spirit comes to Christ (John 6:63-65). Thus, his faith is the gift of God; it is not of works, lest any man should boast (Eph. 2:8-9). All this Christ purchased for us by his sinless life and atoning death.

Secondly, when we speak of the finished work of Christ, we mean that He needed to do nothing more in order to accomplish our redemption. Thus the Psalmist wrote, "The Lord saith unto my Lord, Sit thou at my right hand, until I make thy enemies thy footstool" (Ps. 110:1). In Hebrews we read, "But this man, after he had offered one sacrifice for sins forever, sat down at the right hand of God" (Heb. 10:12). And Paul, speaking of his humiliation said, ". . . he humbled himself, and became obedient unto death, even the death of the cross. Wherefore God also hath highly exalted him . . ." (Phil. 2:8-9).

One of the tragedies of our generation is that many continue to think of Christ as though He continues in the role of the Suffering Servant. He has been exalted! He is seated at the "right hand of majesty" (Heb. 1:3). Who would be aware of his exaltation from the attitude and conduct of some who profess his name. How much contemporary preaching among evangelicals presents a weeping, pleading, powerless Savior. For shame! Indeed, the utterly helpless one who is frequently presented never existed, no, not even in the state of humiliation. Beyond that, He is no longer humbled! "Wherefore thou hast highly exalted him . . . ." He is the Sovereign of the universe who could rightly declare, "All power is given unto me in heaven and in earth" (Matt. 28:18).

Fifthly, we must return to the death of both Christ and the repentant malefactor to observe the vast and vital difference in the meaning of their deaths. The timeless significance of the death of Christ resides in the fact of the atonement. His death was a satisfaction for sin. The death of the malefactor was nothing of the sort. He could not satisfy the justice of God. To the contrary, Christ must die for the sins of the malefactor in order that He might say to him, "Today thou shalt be with me in paradise." But this raises a question. If the wages of sin is death, and if Christ died in the stead of the malefactor, why, then, must the malefactor also die? Our forefathers propounded this very question, "Since, then, Christ died for us, why must we also die?" They replied, "Our death is not a satisfaction for sin, but only a dying to sin (or abolishing of sin) and a passage into eternal life."

Consider this blessed truth. Our death is a dying to sin, or as another translation has it, an "abolishing of sin." Begin with the declaration of Jesus, "I am the resurrection and the life: he that believeth in me, though he were dead, yet shall he live; and whosoever liveth and believeth in me shall never die" (John 11:25-26). Is it true that the believer shall never die? Indeed, it is. The believer shall never suffer death in the deeper, spiritual sense. He will never be separated from God. He shall never be forsaken of God and cast in desolation. He is as a branch grafted again into the vine. The life of God is now his life. He shall never die.

Nonetheless, he does experience physical death. His soul does depart his body to join Christ in Paradise, while his body is laid in the grave. Why? Because God uses physical death to accomplish the complete redemption of man. God does this, first, with respect to the body. The natural body bears the marks of sin, namely susceptibility to disease, injury, deterioration and death. Even when no disease afflicts the body, the passage of the years takes its toll. Ultimately this "earthly house of our tabernacle is dissolved." The infirmities of age are real and often heavy burdens. Many of the saints depart the body with a sigh of relief. They have been released from the achs and pains to which sin has made the body susceptible.

Nor is this all. The natural body is not man's only encumbrance. Though he be "born again," he has yet within him the old nature. The "old man" continues to reside within his breast and afflict him. Throughout his life these two, the new nature and the old, are in conflict. The new man delights in the will of God. The old man is in rebellion against God. A foremost task in the life of the child of God is the mortification, the putting down, the putting to death of the old man, even as he seeks to nurture and develop the growth of the new man. When does the struggle end? At the point of physical death. The old man cannot enter into the kingdom of heaven. Only the new man can enter into the presence of God. Thus physical death becomes the instrument for shedding the old man of sin, the old nature.

Too little do we speak of the blessedness of death in the life of the believer. Occasionally when a loved one has suffered agonizingly, we confess that death was a blessing, but our thoughts are then upon the miseries of the body. This is but part of the affliction sin has brought upon mankind, perhaps even the lesser part. Not only the body of man but his soul bears the afflictions of sin throughout his natural life. Only at death are we relieved of all the havoc wrought by sin.

Two final facts are worthy of our attention. (1) When Jesus said, "Father, into thy hands I commend my Spirit," He was engaged in prayer. He was speaking with God, and whenever one truly speaks with God, that is prayer. Prayer came easily to Jesus in the hour of his death, simply because prayer had always been a real and meaningful part of his life.

Prayer does not come easily to all men in the hour of death. When some men stand before the entrance to the valley of the shadows, they desire to speak with God, as they have never so desired before, only to discover they are unable to speak with God. It is a pitiful experience, because it speaks of a prayerless life. It is a pitiful experience, because it speaks of a soul separated from God — a great gulf fixed between, so that prayer is impossible. What tragedy for any man to stand at the entrance to the valley with these words upon his lips, "Pray for me. I cannot pray."

Here is a rule of the spirit which all should remember. He who prays well in life will also pray well in death. He who prays well in the day of his strength will also pray well in the day of his weakness. What a man has done in the noonday of his life, he will be able to do in the twilight as the shadows gather. If a man would be able to speak with God in that day, let him learn to speak with God now.

(2) Note that the words of Jesus "Father, into thy hands I commend my Spirit," are a quotation from the psalms. You will find them precisely where Jesus did, in the thirty-first psalm. He had read them again and again as a boy and

as a man; and now in the hour of his death, they came forth from his heart and from his lips. He was speaking with God in the language of God.

This, then, is another rule: He who would speak with God would do well to learn the language of God. If a man wishes to speak intelligently with a doctor of medicine, he must learn the language of medicine, of biology, of anatomy, of pathology. If a man wishes to speak intelligently with an engineer, he must learn the language of engineering, of mathematics, of physics, of statics, dynamics and hydraulics.

Someone may reply with the worn cliche, "Language doesn't matter, if one is sincere." We must answer, "If a man is sincere, he will learn the language of God." He who knows the language of God, who is able to use it in life, will not lack for speech when he descends into the valley of the shadows. That which he has done well in life, he will also be able to do well in death.

(3) The words of Christ assume an added depth of meaning when they are placed alongside an Old Testament prayer, "Lord, let me die the death of the righteous..." (Num. 23:10). Though Balaam first uttered this prayer, we need not be concerned with the man or his character. Our attention is directed, rather, to the truth upon which the prayer is predicted. There is a difference in the way men die. The death of the righteous is one. The death of the unrighteous is another. Every child of God may well offer the prayer, "Lord, let me die the death of the righteous."

In the words of Christ, "Father, into thy hands I commend my Spirit," one should observe the ultimate fulfillment of this prayer. When a man stands before the gateway of the valley of the shadows, knowing all of life upon earth is behind, and only the angel of death stands before him — when a man can stand at that place and know that all is well with his soul, because it is in the hands of God — that man can die the death of the righteous. No fear shall enter his heart. No tears shall flow from his eyes. The peace that passes all understanding fills his soul, for his soul is in the hands of God.

How will you die? Will you die the death of the righteous? When you stand before the gateway to the valley, what thoughts will fill your soul? Will you regret the wasted hours, the hours you might have spent in the service of God? Will you fear to stand before the God of all the earth? Or will you be able to say, "Father, into thy hands I commend my Spirit"?

8. Sundown at Noon

"And it was now about the sixth hour, and a darkness came over the whole earth until the ninth hour, the sun's light failing."— Luke 23:44-45

In time past, within the memory of many, virtually all Good Friday services followed a similar pattern. In a large city any number of churches could be expected to conduct midday Good Friday services. One had no need to enquire when any of these services would begin or conclude. All services began at precisely the same hour, twelve o'clock noon, and all services concluded at precisely the same hour, three o'clock.

Some continue to follow this pattern, but many have altered it, usually in the direction of a shorter service. Each year the newspaper announcements indicate that some services begin at twelve-thirty and conclude at two-thirty. Others begin at one o'clock and conclude at three. A few services, usually a distinct minority, begin at the traditional hour of twelve o'clock and continue until the traditional hour of three.

One might conclude that our forefathers in the faith, who insisted the midday service must begin at twelve o'clock and continue until three, were merely arbitrary and boresome. Perhaps they were unnecessarily bound by traditional practice; yet, their position was based on Scriptural grounds. They contended the service must begin at twelve and continue until three, because this was the duration of the period of darkness as Christ hanged upon the cross.

Perhaps this is a pertinent point at which to recognize that the theology of our forefathers in the faith was stronger than our own. Both as ministers in the pulpit and as laymen in the pew, they were, in the main, serious students of the Word of God. Few families failed to own a Bible commentary, and they were read and studied. As a result, they knew what they believed and why they believed it. This accounts, at least in part, for various practices which have been more recently discarded. Many times people of our generation assume they are broadminded when they depart from the ways of their fathers. More to the point in many instances is the fact that the present generation is Biblically ignorant.

The hours of duration of a Good Friday service probably are not significant enough in themselves to merit debate; yet, one might well question how many of our generation realize that the heart of the atonement transpired during the period of the darkness. In the darkness, Christ was forsaken of the Father. In the darkness, He "descended into hell," for this is hell, to be forsaken of the Father. In the darkness He experienced death, not physical death, you understand, but spiritual death, eternal death — which is the state of ultimate, final, complete separation from God.

This undoubtedly is why our forefathers stressed the three hour period of darkness, not so much as a period of time as for what it represented, the heart of the atonement The physical aspect of this event, the falling of the darkness upon the earth, is described in the Gospel record in these words, "And it was about the sixth hour, and a darkness came over all the earth until the ninth hour."

This phenomenon may rightly be called the first of the "miracles of the cross," that is, it was the first in a series of supernatural phenomena which accompanied the death of our Lord. The darkness at midday, the rending of the veil, the quaking of the earth, the opening of the graves, the coming forth of the bodies of the saints after the resurrection of Christ — these we have designated the "miracles of the cross." They are set apart in a special class or category from other miracles recorded in Scripture, the miracles wrought by Christ, the miracles performed by the prophets and the apostles, in that each of them was related directly to the great redemptive work of the cross.

We must understand, all the miracles of Scripture are related to God's redemptive purpose. No miracle was performed merely for its own sake. Nor may we permit secondary considerations to obscure the primary. Frequently, for example, men speak of the "compassion of Jesus" in feeding the hungry, healing the ill, and raising the dead. Is it correct to speak of the compassion of our Lord in relation to such miracles? Of course it is, if his compassion is not permitted to obscure the common denominator which is found in all his miraculous works. What is the common denominator? Each of his miraculous works was an attestation of his deity, and therefore, of the true nature of his mediatorial work (John 14:11).

Similarly, each supernatural event in Scripture was designed by God for its own peculiar contribution to the redemptive program. This fact may be more clearly self-evident in one situation than another. With respect to the miracles Jesus performed, for example, one may see the larger purpose clearly when his enemies would have taken his life prematurely, but He simply passed from their midst untouched. One may see it less clearly in his transformation of water into wine; yet, we must recognize a common denominator in both, namely, a contribution to God's redemptive program.

In addition, the particular miracles we are about to study are directly related to the specific situation of the death and resurrection of Christ. Each of these miracles was a sign given by God, symbolizing, emphasizing and interpreting the redemptive work of Christ. One Biblical scholar comments that these signs came "from the heavens, from the earth, and from under the earth," but each and all of them reveal the meaning and significance of Calvary. So with the first of the "miracles of the cross," the darkness. God was speaking to men through the medium of the darkness.

Three hours Christ hanged upon the cross before the darkness fell. These three hours form a sharp contrast with the three hour period immediately thereafter. The first three hours are filled with activity, the movement of people, the sound of voices. With the darkness came silence. Activity ceased. Movement came to an abrupt halt. The sound of voices is heard no more. To sense the contrast, one must consider the record, both of the first three hours upon the cross and of the three hour period of darkness which followed.

The hubbub of the first three hours was punctuated three times by a word from the lips of Christ. During this period He offered the prayer, "Father, forgive them, for they know not what they do." Then He listened as the thief spoke the mocking words, "Art thou not the Christ? Save thyself and us also." He listened, too, as the other one, the repentant malefactor pled, "Jesus, Lord, remember me when thou comest into thy kingdom." To this man He replied, "Verily I say unto thee, today thou shalt be with me in paradise." Then Jesus made provision for the woman who had served as the instrument of his incarnation. To Mary, his mother, He said, "Woman, behold thy son," and to the beloved apostle John, "Behold thy mother."

Nor was this all. The chief priests were busy voicing their complaint concerning the superscription of the cross which read, "This Is the King of the Jews." They would have had it written, "He Claims to be the King of the Jews." They carried their objection to the governor's palace but to no avail. Meanwhile the soldiers were busy, busy dividing up the garments of the Crucified One, busy casting lots for His seamless robe, looking up now and then from their ill-gotten gains to mock at Him who hanged above them. The multitude had their part also, for we read, they wagged their heads and railed at Him who was suffering the agonies of the cross.

Then — then the scene changed completely. Suddenly the activity and hub-bub at the foot of the cross came to an abrupt halt. Suddenly the voices were stilled. The voice of Christ, the voice of the mocking thief, the voice of the repentant thief — all these became silent. The chief priests, the scribes, the Pharisees, the rulers of the people are heard no more. The soldiers are still. The mocking, reviling multitude is silent. Not a sound may be heard, not a movement anywhere.

Why? Because the darkness, a strange, unnatural darkness had fallen over the earth. There was nought but darkness everywhere, and in the darkness men were still and silent.

One expositor comments dramatically, "There was not a sound in all the earth save one, the spilling of his blood, as it fell drop by drop upon the earth."

No comparable phenomenon has occurred in all recorded history, neither before nor since, except for one which is also recorded in Scripture. This was the ninth plague which preceded the exodus, the plague of darkness which God sent upon the land of Egypt. "God said unto Moses: Stretch out thy hand toward heaven that there may be darkness over all the land of Egypt, even darkness which may be felt. And Moses stretched forth his hand toward heaven; and there was a thick darkness in all the land of Egypt three days; they saw not one another, neither rose anyone from his place for three days . . ." (Exod. 10:21-23).

Neither rose anyone from his place for three days! A darkness which filled men with awe, a darkness which filled men with wonder, a darkness which filled men with fear, so that they did not so much as move from their places while the thick darkness lay upon them. Such was the darkness which fell now, not merely upon the land of Egypt but upon the whole earth as the Son of God hanged upon the cross.

O, some have proposed that the darkness was limited to the area of the cross, say, to the Jerusalem area or to Palestine. Certainly the cross of Christ was the focal point of divine activity that day. And if it were true that the darkness were polarized about the cross, this would in no wise decrease the wonder of it. We are told, however, the cause lay in this, " . . . the sun failing . . ." (Luke 23:45). The King James offers a weak translation, "And the sun was darkened." The American Standard translation is nearer the original. It reads, "The sun's light failing." The Greek original is stronger than either. In the original, it does not merely say, "The sun was darkened," nor merely, "The sun's light failing," but rather, "The sun failing." The sun itself failed! This can mean but one thing. The entire earth was cast into darkness.

Note also the strange, unnatural character of the darkness which lay upon the earth. No comparison may be found in the natural night we experience once each twenty-four hours. The

"natural" night is due to the absence of the sun as the earth
rotates upon its axis. As the earth rotates upon its axis, the
day gradually merges into the night. In some portions of the
earth, the onset of darkness is less perceptible, less apparently
gradual; yet, the night never appears without warning. How
different at Calvary! A moment earlier the sun had blazed in
the heavens. A moment before the earth had been bathed in
the rays of the sun. Now, in a moment of time, the earth was
cast into utter darkness.

Nor could it have been an eclipse of the sun, caused by a
celestial body passing between the sun and the earth. Jesus
was crucified on the Passover. The Passover was always cele-
brated at the full of the moon. And now, twenty centuries
later, astronomers, men who study the celestial bodies and
their movements, declare that an eclipse of the sun is impossible under such conditions. Thus, modern astronomical science
declares that the darkness of the cross cannot be accounted for
by an eclipse of the sun.

More still, the darkness which blotted out the light represented a complete reversal of normal physical action. Or-
dinarily, the light banishes the darkness. If one were to extin-
guish the lights in the sanctuary of a great church, if the entire building were cast into darkness, and then if one were to
light a single small candle, its light would be visible to every
member of the congregation. All the darkness in a great
church building could not put out the light of one small candle. All the darkness in all the world cannot snuff out the
light of one small lamp. How different at the cross! There the
light of the sun was smothered by the darkness at the noon of
the day.

How did it come to pass? To this day no one has produced
a satisfactory answer based on natural causes. To search for an
answer based on natural causes is futile. The darkness of the
cross was not natural; it was supernatural! This was an act of
God. He who separated the light from the darkness in the
time of creation, He who set the stars in their courses, He who
hung the world in space, He who created the sun, now darkened its light and cast the world into utter darkness.

One may note, the darkness at Calvary represents the converse of the extended day of Joshua's time (Joshua 10:12-14). Joshua's armies were engaged in battle. Victory appeared at hand, but evening was approaching, and the enemy might flee in the night. In answer to Joshua's plea, God banished the darkness, and the length of the day was extended. Did God interrupt the rotation of the earth upon its axis? Or did God halt the inter-action of the entire universe? We have no need for an answer to these questions on the mechanics by which God accomplished his purpose. This was as clearly an act of the Sovereign of the universe as was the darkness which fell at midday at Calvary.

Consider, too, apparently nothing else in the universe was disturbed when the darkness fell at Calvary. This may well be considered a testimony to the fact that God Himself was at work. You may recall, when the nation's scientists first began atomic experimentation, when they engaged in the first experiments in thermonuclear fission, they proceeded with great caution. These men said, "The universe is constructed on a principle of balance. We fear our experiments may create a chain reaction which will throw the entire universe out of balance, with fearful, disastrous consequences." They need not have been so fearful at this point. Man's puny efforts, however vast they may seem to human eyes, have not yet unhinged the universe over which a Sovereign God exercises control. Yet here was God disrupting a basic function of the universe, blotting out the sun, and not a blade of grass nor a grain of sand was disturbed on the earth.

What was the meaning of the darkness? We must answer, God sent the darkness as a testimony to the supernatural character of the event which was even then transpiring at Calvary. The darkness was, first, a witness to the deity of Christ and the atoning character of his death. When we are asked for historical proof of the deity of Christ and the atoning character of his death, we turn first to the resurrection. The empty tomb shall forever stand as a witness to the fact that the Crucified One was the Son of God, laying down his life a ransom for many. His resurrection on the third day speaks for itself.

The believers of the Apostolic Age were keenly aware of this fact. The resurrection on the third day was the historic keystone of their faith as it is of ours. In addition, they viewed the darkness which surrounded the cross as further proof of the deity of Christ and the atoning character of his death. When they preached that "God was in Christ reconciling the world unto himself," the pagan scoffers asked, "How can you know?" They replied, "Remember the darkness! Remember the darkness that fell as He hanged upon the cross! Remember the darkness which fell on your land as well as ours! Remember the darkness which covered the earth! Your historians have recorded it. It is written into your own records."

The pagans did know. From father to son the story was related of that strange day, that day like no other, when the whole world had been cast into darkness. Like the blind man who said, "This I know, once I was blind but now I see," so the pagan world was compelled to confess, "This I know, the whole world was cast into darkness that day." Those who were present at the cross in the darkness knew the meaning of this witness, at least some of them did. The centurion knew its meaning, for example, for when the darkness was broken the centurion cried, "Truly, this was the Son of God."

Secondly, the darkness was a testimony to the world-wide significance of the death of Christ. Has it occurred to you how unimportant death may seem, unless it is your loved one who has been taken away? I have pondered this fact. When the funeral service is concluded, and we are making our way to the place of interment, I look out the window of the funeral coach and see the children playing in the schoolyard, the delivery men working their routes, the business men in their commercial establishments, women shopping, streams of traffic. Then I ask myself, "Don't they know? Don't they know the sorrow of those who mourn today?" O, they know in a perfunctory fashion, but no one cares very much.

Sometimes the death of a business or professional man creates a somewhat wider circle of acknowledgment. You may read a notice in the papers: The John Doe Department Store will be closed Tuesday because of the death of Mrs. John Doe.

So the whole city knows. So the employees do not work that day. But nobody cares very much, no one but those who loved Mrs. John Doe. Sometimes, too, a national figure may expire during his term of office, a Lincoln, a McKinley, a Roosevelt. Then the flags are flown at half-mast across the nation. Some daily papers border their front page with black. Public offices are closed. But no one cares very much or very deeply. There is little real mourning.

So it might have been when Christ died, but God would not have it so. God would not permit the world to go on about its business, as though the death of his Son meant nothing to them. All the shops and all the stores in all the world were to be closed that afternoon. No streams of traffic would be permitted to pass along the streets of this world as the Son of God lay down his life. The mothers of families were not to go on with their baking, their cooking, their sewing. Children were not to play in the streets. The fathers of families were not to go on with their business as usual. God caused the whole earth to mourn at the death of His Son by casting the earth into darkness.

O, men were no different then. It would have been "business as usual," had men had their way. The sheer vileness, the depravity of human nature would have sent men, women, and children scurrying on their way as usual, even while the Son of God died. One sees the rebellion, the defiance of man against God at the foot of the cross as they wagged their heads and reviled Him. Then God said, "That's enough. I will not have it! I will not permit this mockery. I will not permit this blasphemy to go on." Thus God cast the earth into darkness, so that the whole earth should mourn at the death of his Son.

It was right that God should do so. Men out of every tongue and tribe and nation had brought this death to pass by their sin. Had He not borne in his own body our sin, He should never have gone to the death of the cross. And now said God, "Let the whole earth mourn, mourn because of their sin which hath brought my Son, Mine Only-Begotten, to the cross."

Thirdly, the darkness was a witness to the inconceivable suffering of Christ. In the suffering of Christ one must distinguish two parts. The first was the suffering men inflicted upon Him, the crown of thorns which brought forth the drops of blood upon his brow, the royal robes of mockery, the leaded whip which lacerated the flesh of his body, the mocking, the scoffing, the spitting in his face, the nails driven into his hands and feet — this was the work of men. But this was not all! One might rightly say, it was the lesser part of his suffering. The greater part of his suffering, the inconceivably excruciating portion of his suffering, came directly from the hand of God. The beating, the whipping, the nails — these were as nothing when the hand of God's wrath was laid directly upon Him. The prophet foretold it. "Stricken, smitten of God and afflicted," said the prophet, and so He was — smitten of God.

One may perceive a foreshadowing of this suffering in Gethsemane. The enemy had not yet discovered Him in the garden. The eight had been left to wait at the garden gate. The three who came with Him were told to wait, as He moved off about a "stone's cast" away. There He knelt in the garden. No human hand was laid upon him. No human finger touched him; yet, he sweat as it were great drops of blood falling to the ground. How shall we explain it? Smitten of God! This is the only conceivable answer. Smitten of God! The hand of God was laid upon Him. The hand of justice and judgment crushed from him the bloody sweat of the garden.

In Gethsemane the disciples were not permitted to come all the way, not even Peter, James or John, but they were permitted to know what happened there, and they were permitted to record it for us. By contrast, even the record is silent about Calvary in the darkness. No human eye was permitted to see what transpired there. No human tongue was permitted to tell. No human pen was to leave a record of the awful fury of the wrath of God and the inconceivable suffering of Christ.

Someone has written, God dropped the cloak of darkness about the cross, so that the sufferings of Christ should not be further exposed to human view. Perhaps, but it was more than that. No man could bear to see what happened at Calvary in the darkness. You ask, "What did happen there? What happened in the darkness?" I do not know. I do not want to know.

I do not ever want to know. Whatever it was, out there in the darkness, it brought forth the soul-searing cry of the ages, "My God, my God, why hast thou forsaken me?" But some will know. In that last great day, when those who have remained in their rebellion and defiance against God are cast into the bottomless pit, they shall know. They shall be cast into the outer darkness forever. Out of the darkness, we are told, shall come their weeping, their wailing, their gnashing of teeth.

This, after all, is why He went out into the darkness, so that we who believe on his name shall never be called upon to enter the darkness of lost souls. He carried our sins out into the darkness and left them there. He went where the justice of God demands that every sinner shall go. He went out into the darkness in our stead. And therefore, God declares to us, "Now is the acceptable time," and again, "Today is the day of salvation." Why now? Why today? Because the night cometh, and for those who have not found peace with God, there is only the darkness forever.

9. The Rent Veil: His Flesh

"And, behold, the veil of the temple was rent in twain from the top to the bottom." — Matt. 27:51

We are well acquainted with the "Seven Words of the Cross." Were you aware, however, that Jesus spoke yet once more from the cross, that He spoke, not seven times but eight? Were you to be unaware of this fact, it should not be thought surprising. Think back, if you will, when did you last hear a sermon on the eighth "word" from the cross? Though the eighth "word" from the cross receives scant attention, it cannot be dismissed as though it were irrelevant or incidental. On the contrary, it was the eighth "word" from the cross which might be said to have "rocked the world."

If you were to ask, "Why does the eighth 'word' from the cross receive so little attention?" one might answer, "Because it was no 'word' at all." Does this seem contradictory? We mean, it was not an intelligible word; it was not a recognizable word. It was a cry, a shout, which was unintelligible to human ears; yet it holds deep significance when it is viewed as part of a sequence of amazing, supernatural events which transpired about the cross as the Savior lay down his life a ransom for many. Only as we view the skein of supernatural events which followed the cry from the cross will we understand why this may be called the cry which "rocked the world."

The Biblical record is short and concise, just these words, "And Jesus cried again with a loud voice, and yielded up his Spirit. And behold, the veil of the temple was rent in two from the top to the bottom; and the earth did quake, and the rocks were rent; and the tombs were opened; and many bodies of the saints who had fallen asleep were raised..." (Matt. 27:50-52 ASV).

We must turn first to the rending of the veil. This may be termed the second of the "miracles of the cross," because it was preceded by the unnatural darkness at noonday. Unfortunately, the miraculous character of the rending of the veil has, apparently, escaped the attention of many. A young man in a Bible class made the remark, "This was not a miracle. The earthquake caused the veil to be rent." This appears to be a rather common assumption, namely, that the rending of the veil was a "natural" consequence of the quaking of the earth. Consequently, we should pay heed to several considerations which point to the miraculous or supernatural character of the rending of the veil.

First, if one reads the Scriptural record with special attention toward the time sequence of events, he will discover the veil was rent *before* the earth began to quake. In order of occurrence, the rending of the veil *preceded* the quaking of the earth. If there be anything of cause and effect among the events which transpired about the cross in that hour, the cry of Christ preceded both the rending of the veil and the earthquake. The cry from the lips of Christ would seem to have set the whole pattern in motion. The echo of his cry had not died away when the veil was rent, the earth trembled, the rocks were rent, and the graves were opened. This is why it has been said, whether figuratively or literally, this is "the cry which rocked the world." This much cannot be denied, the reverberations of that cry have not died away after twenty centuries.

Secondly, when the earth did quake and tremble, the temple was undamaged. We shall study this phenomenon more closely at another time and discover that this was the most unusual earthquake of all time. Though the earthquake was of such force and proportions that the rocks were rent asunder and tombs were wrenched open, no property damage was left in its wake. Specifically, the temple, the one structure with which we need to be concerned, stood undamaged. Neither sacred history nor secular history provide any indication that the temple was damaged by the quaking of the earth. Thus the temple, wherein hung the veil, was left unscathed. No walls crumbled away to wrench the veil part. No timbers fell to strike the veil. When the earth ceased to tremble, the temple bore no marks of stress or damage.

Thirdly, this was a loose-hanging veil. It was not bound in place. On the contrary, the veil was supported by golden eyelets upon a rod; thus, it was permitted free movement upon the rod from which it hung. If, therefore, the temple had been destroyed, had it been demolished, had it crumbled into a heap of rubble, it is doubtful whether the veil would have been rent. Had the temple been demolished, the veil would have suffered to be certain. In all probability it would have been covered with rubble, soiled and dirtied. Even so, it is highly improbable that the veil would have been rent. Why? The freedom of movement, insured by the golden eyelets, would permit no stress or tensions upon the material of the veil.

No, the veil was not ripped or rent asunder by natural forces. In truth, the more one studies the Scriptural record, the more certain he becomes that no "natural" explanation can be offered for the rending of the veil. This was an act of God, an immediate act of God. If you were to ask, "How did God cause the veil to be rent?" the answer must be, "Without visible or instrumental means."

O, God might have done otherwise. He might have sent a thunderbolt crashing through the skies. He might have sent the lightning flashing down, and with its searing heat, He might have rent the veil in twain. Again, God might have sent Michael, the archangel of the sword. With one slash of his sword Michael would have rent the veil in twain, even from the top unto the bottom. Still again, God might have sent the Cherubim who were stationed at the garden gate in Eden, the Cherubim with the sword that "turned every which way." There would have been a fitness to it, had God sent the Cherubim who restrained Adam from re-entering the garden after his sin. The first Adam created a barrier between God and man by his sin. Now the Second Adam abolished the barrier by reconciling man to God. It would have been fitting, therefore, but God did not choose to send the Cherubim of the flaming sword. Nor did God employ any visible instrumentality to rend the veil.

How, then, did God cause the veil to be rent in twain, even from the top to the bottom? You must remember, this is the God who called the worlds into being with a word from his Sovereign lips. You must remember, this is the God who set the sun and the moon in the heavens with a word from his lips. This is the God who set the stars in their orbits with a word from his lips. For He spoke, and it was done. He commanded, and it was brought forth. This, then, is the relationship between the cry of Christ from the cross and the rending of the veil. The Scriptures declare, "And Jesus cried again with a loud voice . . . and, behold, the veil of the temple was rent in twain from the top to the bottom." He spoke, and it was done! A word from his lips, and the veil was rent in twain, even from the top to the bottom!

To grasp the significance of this act of God, one must comprehend the meaning of the veil. The temple was, of course, the successor to the tabernacle. Now, some aspects of the temple differed from those of the tabernacle, but the veil hung in both. And the meaning of the veil was the same in each. Therefore, to understand the meaning of the veil, we return to the original tabernacle, for which God Himself drew the plan and wrote the specifications, delivering them to Moses.

The tabernacle was divided into three areas or compartments known as the Outer Court, the Holy Place and the Holy of Holies. Both the Holy Place and the Holy of Holies stood within the Outer Court. The innermost sanctuary, the Holy of Holies, could be entered only by first passing through the Holy Place. The people, the congregation if we were to employ current terminology, were permitted only in the Outer Court. They were not permitted to enter or even to see within the Holy Place, for a veil was hung between, cutting off their vision from the inner chamber. Only the priests were permitted to enter the Holy Place. They entered it daily to carry on their priestly ministrations. Even the priests, however, were not permitted to enter the Holy of Holies. Nor were the priests permitted to look into the Holy of Holies. Their vision was cut off by a second veil which hung before the entrance to the Holy of Holies.

Within the Holy of Holies was the ark of the covenant, with its golden cover, the mercy seat. Within were the cherubim. Within was the cloud of glory, the Shekinah, the presence of God. Into this place only the high priest might come. The high priest entered the Holy of Holies but once each year, and then only after he had been properly cleansed according to the ceremonial law.

In view of these considerations, note the significance of the veil. The first veil, which shut the congregation off from the Holy Place, was a visible, tangible barrier, restraining the lay membership of the Old Testament church from approaching the presence of God because of their sin. The second veil barred even the priest from the Holy of Holies wherein dwelt the presence of God. The second veil, therefore, restrained even those who were ordained to the priesthood from entering into the immediate presence of God. Though they were called of God to a sacred office, they were men, mere men — men who were sinful and guilty. It was this veil, the second veil, which was rent in twain, even from the top to the bottom, that veil which had barred God's people from his immediate presence.

The veil stood as a very real symbol of the barrier which sin erects between the sinner and God. Precisely because He is a Holy God, sinful man cannot enter into his presence. The veil speaks of a most disastrous consequence of sin. Sin separates the sinner from God. Perhaps we should say, more correctly, the holiness of God, reacting against sin, erects a barrier, a wall, an impregnable wall between God and man.

Adam discovered this truth in the dawn of human history. No sooner had he fallen into sin than he was expelled from the garden wherein he had walked and talked with God. No longer was there any place in the garden paradise for Adam. He was driven forth from its gates, and the gates were forever after closed to him. Before the gate stood the cherubim of the flaming sword. Every which way turned the sword, denying

Adam entrance to the garden wherein he had known the presence of God.

The unbeliever may not recognize the disastrous consequences of separation from the presence of God. He may say to himself falsely, "I have gotten along rather well without God for many a year," because he fails to recognize his moment to moment dependence upon God. True, he does not enjoy communion with God as does the believer, but neither has he been cast into desolation by God. He is separated from God but not totally cut off. He has no present conception of what it means to be totally cut off from God. That awaits him in the other world. Were he to come to Calvary, he might learn the fearfulness of being utterly shut out from God. Were he to stand at the foot of the cross in the darkness, that awful darkness which blanketed the earth, that awful darkness wherein there was nought but silence, he might learn. He would hear the cry that came forth from the lips of Christ, the agonizing cry which has come piercing down through the ages, "My God, my God, why hast thou forsaken me?" This is what it means to be utterly cast out from the presence of God.

Only when the awful suffering of the cross was completed, only when the justice of God was satisfied, only when the wrath of God had been expended, only when Christ could say, "It is finished" — then He cried with a loud voice, and the veil was rent in twain.

What did it signify, this rending of their veil? First, the rending of the veil was God's announcement that the price of sin had been paid. The veil was a symbol of man's unfitness to come into the presence of God. Sin had erected the veil, but now sin was done away. He had borne in his own body our sin. He had carried it out into the darkness and left it there. Since sin had been removed, the barrier must also be removed; thus, the veil was rent in twain. This, therefore, was God's testimony that the price of sin had been paid. This was God's declaration that divine justice had been satisfied.

You may have witnessed a similar situation in connection with commercial transactions. A business man borrows a sum of money from a bank. He signs a note for the amount he has received. Ninety days later, he repays the principal plus interest. The loan officer takes out the note which the borrower signed three months before. He may give the note to the borrower, or he may simply tear up the note and destroy it. It no longer has value or meaning. The debt has been paid. So God took the veil. For centuries the veil stood as a sign of man's indebtedness to God. Now the debt had been paid. And God took the veil and rent it in twain, even from the top to the bottom.

The last sound Jesus uttered attests to this fact. This was the cry which was no word at all. This was the cry which rent the veil, set the earth to trembling, rent the rocks asunder, and opened the graves of the saints. This was the cry of victory. The battle was done. The victory was won. The atonement had been accomplished. The price had been paid. With this cry, the veil was rent in twain. The very cry which announced that the price of sin had been paid rent the veil in twain. Even as He put away sin once and forever, the veil which had shut man off from God was done away.

The Jewish priesthood recognized the significance of this sign as we scarcely can. That many of them realized its significance, we shall see in a moment. It was three o'clock in the afternoon. As the hour struck, many things came to pass. The darkness lifted. The cry of victory burst forth from the lips of Christ. The veil was rent. Take note of the hour; it is important. At three o'clock in the afternoon, the sacrifices were begun. This meant the entire company of the priests would be standing in the Holy Place; indeed, they would be standing before the veil at the altar of sacrifice. This is precisely where God wanted them. The hour had been fixed in eternity before time began. Those who were most directly responsible for the death of Christ were to see the rending of the veil. As they stood before the veil, prepared to engage in their priestly ministrations, suddenly they heard the cry in the distance and stood transfixed as the veil was rent in twain before their very eyes. For the first time their eyes peered into the Holy of Holies wherein dwelt the presence of God.

They would testify that no human hand had touched the veil. They would testify that no wall had crumbled. They would testify that no timber had fallen. They would testify that God Himself had rent the veil. They had seen it! They knew its significance. O, yes, they knew what it meant! How can we be certain? Because, we read, as soon as the gospel was proclaimed after Pentecost, " . . . a great company of the priests were obedient to the faith" (Acts 6:7) .

The seemingly impossible came to pass. These were the men who had dealt with the betrayer, paying Judas "blood money" to lead them to Christ. These were the men who sat in judgment upon him before the high court of the Jews. These were the men who had aroused the multitude to shout, "Crucify him! Crucify him!" Now they had entered the fold. They were obedient to the faith. How could it be? These were men who had heard the cry in the distance, and with that cry, they had seen the veil rent in twain. They knew the meaning of the rending of the veil. The Messiah of prophecy, the long promised Redeemer, had come. He had done away with sin.

These men had not been convinced by the miracles of Jesus. Though He stilled the waters of the sea, though He healed the sick, the lame, the blind, and the halt, though He raised the very dead, they would not believe. But now they knew! With their own ears they had heard the piercing cry from the cross, and with their own eyes they had seen the veil rent in twain. They knew that sin had been put away. "And a great company of the priests became obedient to the faith!"

Secondly, the rending of the veil was God's announcement that the One Great High Priest had done his work, and the work being done, the high-priestly office was forever done away among men. Only the high priest had been permitted to enter beyond the second veil, but now the veil was done away. So we read in Hebrews (6:20) that God hath made Him (that is, Christ) an High Priest forever, and again, that He accomplished by the sacrifice of Himself what all the other sacrifices of all ages could not do (Heb. 10:11-12) . He had paid the price of sin!

In this connection, we should recall the dual capacity in which Christ functioned at the cross. We are quite aware that He was Himself the sacrifice. As such, He took our place in bearing the wrath of God upon sin. At the same time, He was likewise the High Priest who executed the sacrifice of the cross. As such, He sacrificed Himself. This He made clear when He said, "No man taketh my life. I lay it down of myself." Sometimes we refer to this fact, because men must know that the crucified Christ was not the helpless victim of the cross, but rather, He gave Himself freely to the death of the cross. Now, however, we must see Him as the one great High Priest for another reason. We must see Him as that One Great High Priest who was capable of executing the one perfect sacrifice, and by that one perfect sacrifice, He eliminated the office of the earthly high priest forever.

Why? Because the high priest had a specific task to perform, a particular function to fulfill. He sprinkled the blood of animals upon the mercy seat. Why? Because the blood of animals could satisfy the justice of God? By no means! The sprinkling of the blood of animals simply pointed toward the shedding of the Savior's blood. Now the blood of the Savior had been shed. With the shedding of his blood, the price of sin had been paid. Nothing more remained to be done, and the task being completed, the office was abolished.

Again, once only the high priest was permitted to pass beyond the veil into the presence of God. Now the veil had been rent, destroyed, abolished, done away. No longer was man barred from the presence of God. All men, that is all who are "in Christ," might come into the presence of God for themselves. We need no representative to appear before God in our stead. We may enter into the very presence of God for ourselves.

Our purpose is not constantly to point to the errors of the church of Rome. At the same time, we must certainly remind ourselves and our children why we do not have a special priesthood in the Protestant church. This was done away in the death of our Lord. The priest is one who stands between man and God. Now, however, there is but "one mediator between God and Men, the man, Christ Jesus" (I Tim. 2:5). We must understand, further, this is not a mere fine point of theology which we can afford to dismiss as though it were without consequence. To the contrary, this lies at the heart of our faith. For any man to usurp, if that were possible, the place of Christ and take to himself the title of a priest, in that sense, is not only presumptuous but it does grave dishonor to Christ and to his death at Calvary.

We can commit no sin more grave than this, to dishonor our Lord and his death. We should give thanks daily for the grace of God which raised up the Reformers, men such as Luther and Calvin who, at the risk of their very lives, returned to us the pure doctrines of the Word of God. To suggest that we are "not very different" from the church of Rome is to do grave dishonor, not only to these men, but much more serious, to our Lord and to his death upon the cross.

More still, we do not believe in a special priesthood, because the Bible teaches that every believer is a priest before God. So we read, "Ye are . . . a royal priesthood . . . that ye may shew forth the excellencies of him who called you out of darkness into his marvelous light" (I Peter 2:9). This is a consideration of no little significance. We have said that we do not believe in a special priesthood, but we most assuredly do believe in a general priesthood or, as Martin Luther put it, a universal priesthood of believers.

This points to a third aspect of the rent veil. The rending of the veil was God's announcement that the way was now open for all the redeemed to enter into the presence of God. This is also what we mean by the priesthood of all believers. Everyman, that is every believer, may enter into the presence of his God. Thus we read, "Having therefore, brethren, boldness to enter into the holy place by the blood of Jesus, by the way which he dedicated for us, by a new and living way, through the veil, that is to say, his flesh; and having a great high priest over the house of God, let us draw near with a true heart in fullness of faith" (Heb. 10:19-22).

This statement brings to us the full significance and meaning of the rending of the veil. Here we learn that the veil symbolizes His flesh. By his broken body and by his shed blood, the veil was rent in twain. This is what Christ wrought at Calvary. He destroyed the barrier between God and man. He opened the way for man to return to the presence of God.

This significance of this event, what Christ wrought at Calvary in behalf of man, caused the writer of Hebrews to cry out, "How shall we escape, if we neglect [this] so great salvation?" (Heb. 2:3). This must always be our question to men, "How shall you escape, if you neglect this, O so great salvation?" What will you say to God in that last great day, if you do despite unto the Son of God in this, the day of salvation?

Jesus spoke of this matter in a parable. He told of a householder who had planted a vineyard and then journeyed into another country, letting out his vineyard to husbandmen (Luke 20:9-18). When the time of harvest was come, the owner sent his servants to receive the fruit of the vineyards, but the husbandmen treated them shamefully, beating one, killing another, and stoning a third. Then the owner said to himself, "I will send my beloved son: it may be they will reverence him. ..." But the husbandmen said to themselves, "This is the heir. Come, let us kill him, that the inheritance may be ours." And they took him, cast him forth out of the vineyard and slew him.

Then Jesus asked, "What therefore shall the Lord of the vineyard do unto them?" They answered, "He will come and destroy those husbandmen. ..." Some of you will say, "This is what the Jews did to Jesus." Ah, yes, so they did. And so do you, you who do not acknowledge that He is your Lord and King, you who refuse to worship and bow down. "Ye crucify him afresh daily," saith the Word of God, and so you do.

But what will you say in that day when He cometh? How shall you escape, if you neglect this great salvation? Will you stand in the darkness with them who cry, "Lord, Lord, open to us," only to hear Him say, "I know you not"? Will you cry for the rocks and the mountains to fall upon you, only to discover there is no escape? Will you plead, along with the rich man, for a drop of water upon your parched tongue, only to be told there is a great gulf fixed between? How shall you escape, if you neglect this great salvation? By the mercies of God, we beseech you brethren, be ye reconciled to God.

10. The Earth Did Quake

"And behold, the veil of the temple was rent in twain from the top to the bottom; and the earth did quake."—Matt. 27:51

The time was three o'clock in the afternoon. Our Lord had already spoken his "seventh word" from the cross. This was the prayer, "Father, into thy hands I commend my Spirit." Then Matthew records, "And Jesus cried again with a loud voice . . . , and behold the veil of the temple was rent in two from the top unto the bottom; and the earth did quake, and the rocks were rent; and the tombs were opened; and many of the bodies of the saints which slept were raised. . . . "

This statement directs our attention to the event which we have denominated the "third miracle of the cross," the quaking of the earth as Christ lay down his life at Calvary. We have termed it the third miracle of the cross, because it was preceded by the rending of the veil. The rending of the veil, in turn, was preceded by the cloak of darkness which blanketed the earth for a period of three hours beginning at the noon of the day.

"The earth did quake," writes Matthew. "And why should this be thought unusual," someone may ask, "since earthquakes are a relatively common phenomenon?" True, history provides numerous accounts of earthquakes. The Roman Empire experienced a series of severe quakes but a generation later, that is, but a generation after the death of Christ, between the years A.D. 60 and A.D. 80. Much more recently Costa Rica, Japan, and the state of California have each been visited by disastrous quakes. To say that the earthquake at the cross was a miracle, is not to disregard or depreciate the fact that various sectors of the earth have been visited by quakes from time to time. Nor do we dispute that other earthquakes were born out of so-called natural causes. To put it another way, an explanation can be provided for them in terms of physico-geological causes.

Why, then, do we view the earthquake at the cross as a miracle? For a number of reasons. First, an earthquake of any proportions causes large-scale damage and destruction. Buildings are shattered and crumbled. Lives are lost. The California earthquake of 1906 will serve as an example. Virtually the entire city of San Francisco was destroyed. The Japanese earthquake in 1923 provides another example. Damage, destruction and loss of life were almost incalculable. By contrast, the earthquake at the cross was most severe as we shall see in a moment; yet, the Scriptural record gives no indication that a single building was destroyed. Neither, apparently, did any loss of life result.

The severity of the earthquake at the cross may be ascertained from the record. We discover, first, the very rocks were rent. This was not a mere tremor in the earth. We should note this fact, because minor tremors occur in the earth with relative frequency. Many are so mild, the public is unaware of their occurrence. If they are reported at all, the daily press may print a short back-page item indicating that a tremor was recorded on the seismograph of this or that university. By contrast, major quakes are relatively rare, and the quake at the cross was of major proportions.

Only a serious convulsion in the earth's surface could have caused the rocks to be rent. You see, an earthquake consists in a movement of the earth's surface. All factors involved have not been ascertained even at the present time by the physical geologists who study such matters. Internal fires, intense heat within the interior of the earth is commonly regarded as a factor. The shrinkage of the earth's cover or surface is also viewed as a related, contributing factor. Whatever the causes may be, portions of the earth's surface are moved and displaced.

Sometimes this displacement is vertical. In the quake of 1899 portions of the Alaskan coast line were elevated forty-seven feet above their previous level. Visualize, if you can, your home suddenly being catapulted upward, far beyond the roof-tops of your neighbors' houses, and you will perceive what is involved. Sometimes the displacement is lateral. In the California quake of 1906 portions of the earth's surface were moved twenty-one feet from their previous position. If you can visualize houses, buildings, and the land beneath them suddenly being picked up and deposited in another location, you will see what this means.

You will also perceive that immeasurable forces are at work in an earthquake. The heaviest bulldozer with the largest blade could not accomplish in a year what an earthquake will do in a matter of moments. The most powerful thermo-nuclear bombs yet devised, bombs which are reputed to be capable of sinking an entire island into the depths of the sea, cannot match the destructive force of a number of quakes which have occurred in the earth.

The earthquake at the cross was tremendous in its power. The rocks were rent! Only a student of geology would recognize the full implications of this fact. First, this would seem to signify a vertical displacement of the earth's surface, a displacement similar to that which occurred on the Alaskan coast when a span of the coastal area was boosted forty-seven feet above its previous level. In a vertical shift such as this, geologists declare, the rocks would be literally sheared apart by the force of the movement of the earth's surface.

More than that. Tombs were opened. This speaks to the severity of the quake in another direction or plane, that is, laterally. The Palestine area, and the Jerusalem district in particular, is rocky country. If you have traveled through Pennsylvania, Tennessee, Colorado or similar areas, you will recall that even the roads in some places must be blasted through solid rock. The surface of the earth is not the dirt or loam to which we are accustomed in the Midwest. The earth's surface is comprised of solid rock, stretching for many miles in every direction. The Jerusalem area is similar.

of the malefactors be broken to hasten their death. Thus the three crosses stood undisturbed on Calvary's hill.

The purpose of God in creating this unusual situation must be recognized of course. Had this been a natural quake, with the crosses cast about, with buildings crumbling, with attendant combustion and destruction, the bodies might well have been buried in the rubble and debris. It is quite possible that the bodies might not have been recovered. This has been common experience in similar catastrophes. For all the effects at reclamation and recovery, many bodies of the deceased have never been recovered after each of the great quakes of which we have record. As for the bodies of the two malefactors, perhaps it would have made little difference, but the body of Christ must be preserved. The death of Christ must be certified above and beyond question or dispute. His body must also be placed in the tomb. The tomb must be sealed. The tomb must be guarded — so that for all generations to come, the fact of our Lord's death and resurrection would be known, proved and certified.

Secondly, the temple was undisturbed. This in itself is a wonder of no small proportions. In 1910 when Costa Rica was struck by an earthquake, the Carnegie Palace of Peace was nearing completion at Cartago, Costa Rica. It was a reinforced steel structure, not basically different in construction than some of the finest buildings being erected in America today; yet, that great building was utterly demolished, reduced to a heap of rubble by the quake. When the rocks were rent, and the tombs were wrenched open in Jerusalem, however, the temple stood undisturbed.

The plan and purpose of God in this circumstance should also be noted. The veil had been rent in twain just before the earthquake struck. It must continue to hang in plain view in the temple as a witness to the meaning and significance of the sacrifice of Christ upon the cross. In the infinite wisdom of the divine plan, no detail is disregarded. The smallest particularia is planned and executed with infinite care. The rent veil must continue to hang undisturbed. Therefore, though

Because of this condition, the bodies of the deceased w
not buried in the earth as is common practice among
Tombs were hewn out of the stone of the hillsides and cli
This is also true of certain areas in our own country, y
know. In certain areas of the southeastern United States, gra
must be blasted out of the rock. So it was in Palestine. Th
when we read that the tombs were opened, we must und
stand that the force of the earthquake was so great the so
rock tombs were ruptured.

This, by geological standards, speaks of a lateral displac
ment of the earth's surface. A lateral displacement of th
earth's surface would account for the fact that the tombs wer
literally wrenched open. Significantly, the graves were opened
much as if someone had opened the cover of a box, so tha
the bodies lay in plain view; yet, the bodies were undisturbed
This fact demonstrates that a lateral displacement accom
panied the vertical displacement. A vertical displacement at
these points would have moved the bodies, perhaps violently,
so that the bodies would have been catapulated out of their
graves. Thus, we conclude, a lateral displacement was necessary to open the tombs in precisely this manner, even as a
vertical displacement was necessary to rend the rocks.

Someone may ask, "Is not this true of all earthquakes? Do
not all earthquakes consist in either a vertical or a lateral displacement of the earth's surface, or of both a vertical and lateral displacement together?" This is true, but some unexplained facts remain in connection with the earthquake at the
cross. The disruption, the damage, if one could call it that,
was selective. The earth was shaken, the rocks were rent, the
tombs were opened, *but,* and note this carefully, nothing else
was disturbed!

The three crosses on Calvary's hill, for example, were not
displaced. Imagine it, if you can. The earth quaking, rocks
rent, tombs opened, but the three crosses on Calvary's hill
stood undisturbed. When the quaking had subsided, when the
last tremor had died away, the three crosses were found to be
standing just as they had before. Only later would the spear
be plunged into the side of Christ. Only later would the legs

the earth should quake, though rocks should be rent, though graves should be opened, the temple must stand unscathed.

Thirdly, only selected graves were opened. If you will read the passage carefully, you will discover the graves were not opened indiscriminately. The opened graves were those of the saints. If this were merely a case of some graves being opened while others remained closed, one might assume that this was merely the vaguary of the disruption caused by the quake. But these were selected graves! The graves which were opened were those of the saints, of the elect, of believers, of men of faith. The graves which remained closed were those of unbelievers.

Think of it! Here was a tomb in which had been laid to rest the body of a child of God. The tomb was opened by the quake. Beside it was another tomb, hewn out of the same rock in the same hillside. That tomb contained the physical remains of an unbeliever. That tomb remained closed.

When one adds all these facts together, he must perceive immediately that this was not an ordinary earthquake, one which can be explained in the same terms as other earthquakes. Rocks were rent asunder, but the cross of Christ stood undisturbed in the midst of the upheaval. The earth quaked and trembled, but the temple of the Lord stood unmoved and undisturbed. Tombs were wrenched open but not all tombs, only the tombs of the saints. This earthquake was unlike any other in all history. This quaking of the earth's surface was designed by God to fulfill a particular purpose at a particular time in a particular way.

God may have brought this phenomenon to pass by a sheer act of his will, that is, without the use of intermediate instrumentalities. He may have brought it to pass by a mere word from his lips. If so, this fact need occasion no difficulty, either of faith or of intellect, for the believer. We know Him as the God who called the worlds into being by the might of his power. It is written of our God, "He spake, and it was done," and again, "He commanded, and it was brought forth." Further, what we believe concerning his creative activity, we likewise believe concerning the providential government which He continues to exercise over the whole creation. If the

Sovereign of the universe so wills, a mere word from his lips would cause the earth to tremble.

On the other hand, God may have used what we term to be "natural causes," though if He did, He controlled and directed them in an unusual and unique manner. We understand that the hand of God always lies behind so-called natural causes. We should realize that the hand of God lay beneath the "natural causes" which brought an earthquake to San Francisco, just as surely as the hand of God wrought an earthquake that long ago day at Calvary. In either case, we cannot disregard the unusual and unique characteristics of the quaking of the earth in Palestine which causes us to regard this quake as a miracle.

Thus, we readily confess, God may have used "natural causes," employing them in an unusual manner, to produce the mysterious quaking of the earth that day. God may have been preparing both the interior and the surface of the earth in that area for centuries, shaping the various components so that they would act in a particular way at a particular time. The means, if any, which God employed to bring the quake to pass is not the issue of immediate importance to us. This much is indisputably clear: God so controlled the quaking of the earth that not a portion of its surface, not a rock, not a stone, not a blade of grass, not a particle of dust was moved, unless it contributed to the purpose of God in bringing the earthquake to pass.

What, then, was God's purpose in causing the earth to quake? Several answers to this question appear. (1) The earthquake was a visual demonstration of the presence of God at Calvary. If the scene at Calvary with the earthquake, the rending of the rocks, the opening of the tombs, and the ultimate raising of the dead was awe-inspiring and fearsome, other scenes in Scripture are scarcely less so. When God appeared before the prophet Elijah on Mount Horeb, we read, a great and strong wind rent the mountains and broke in pieces the rocks before the Lord. The wind was followed by an earthquake. The earthquake was followed by a fire. Then spoke the voice of God (I Kings 19:11-12). So, too, when God came to Moses upon Mount Sinai, presenting him with the decalogue, graven upon tablets of stone. The Scriptures record that God descended upon the Mount in a fire. The whole of Mount Sinai smoked as the smoke of a great furnace, and the mount quaked greatly (Exod. 19:18).

What is the meaning of all this, the fearsome signs and wonders which occurred at Mount Sinai at the giving of the law, at Mount Horeb when God spoke with Elijah, and at Mount Calvary when the Son of God lay down His life for our redemption? We need not engage in speculation or conjecture. Scripture provides its own interpretation, for the Psalmist wrote, "The earth shook . . . even Sinai itself was moved at the presence of God" (Ps. 68:8). This is the meaning of the fearsome signs, the presence of God. When Sinai trembled at the giving of the law, it did so because God was present there. When Horeb trembled as God spoke to Elijah, it did so because God was present there. When Calvary trembled at the death of Christ, it did so because God was present there. This was God the Father, the great, eternal, sovereign God present at the death of His Son.

(2) The trembling of the earth was a testimony that God, not man, had erected the cross of Christ at Calvary. Did these men, these little men of whom the Scriptures say, "From the dust thou wast taken, and to the dust thou shalt return" — did they think for one moment they could have sentenced the Son of God to the death of the cross, except it were foreordained of God? Did these men, these little men of whom the Scriptures say, "Like the grass of the field which today is and tomorrow is cast into the oven for burning" — did they think for one moment they could have impaled the Eternal Son of Eternal God upon a cross, except it were predestined of God from before the foundations of the world?

Ah, no, this was God's announcement that He who framed the worlds and brought them into being, He who is able to shake the universe with a breath from His sovereign lips, had permitted these things to come to pass. Nay more, He had foreordained that they should come to pass for the redemption of the world.

This was God's method for announcing to the world that the words of the Son were true when He said, "No man taketh away my life; I lay it down of myself." This was God's stamp of approval upon the prayer of Christ in Gethsemane, when amidst the drops of blood He prayed, "Let this cup pass from me; nevertheless, not my will but thine be done." For this was the will of God, that the Son should lay down His life a ransom for many.

Peter testified to this fact as he preached to the multitude on Pentecost. We hear him say, "Him, being delivered up by the determinate counsel and foreknowledge of God, ye have taken, and by wicked hands have crucified and slain" (Acts 2:23). Yes, men had taken Him with wicked hands and nailed his blessed body to the cross, but his death came to pass, because, and only because of the determinate counsel and foreknowledge of God. And the fearful things which came to pass at the cross were God's announcement that no man could have crucified the Son, except The Father had ordained it so.

Peter spelled out the matter in greater detail a moment later when he said, "For of a truth against thy holy child Jesus, whom thou hast anointed, both Herod and Pontius Pilate, with the Gentiles and the people of Israel, were gathered together, For to do whatsoever thy hand and thy counsel determined before to be done" (Acts 4:27-28). Who determined that Christ should die at Calvary? God had willed it so from eternity! And now God shook the earth to tell men that his purpose and his good pleasure were accomplished at Calvary that day. Not the purposes of men, but the purposes of God were accomplished at Calvary.

(3) The trembling of the earth at Calvary was God's declaration of the scope of the redemptive program. So often when we speak of the cross, of the shedding of the blood of Christ, we think only in terms of the souls of men, or smaller still, of our own souls. This is not illegitimate. We may rightfully think in these terms, for it is written, "This is a faithful saying, and worthy of all acceptation, that Christ Jesus came

into the world to save sinners," and Paul added the personal declaration, " . . . of whom I am chief."

Even so, God's purpose was grander than that, and Christ accomplished far more than that at Calvary. We fail to recognize the scope, either of sin or of grace, if we assume only man is in need of redemption. Man is not alone under the curse of sin. We read that the whole earth was cursed because of man's sin. Not only man but the very earth on which man dwells is under the curse of God upon sin. This is why Paul wrote, "The whole creation groaneth [looking forward to that last day] for the manifestation of the sons of God, for," wrote Paul, "the creation itself shall be delivered from the bondage of corruption into the glorious liberty of the children of God" (Rom. 8:19-21).

Peter provides further detail in his second epistle where we read, "The day of the Lord will come . . . in . . . which the heavens shall pass away with a great noise, and the elements shall be dissolved with fervent heat, and the earth and the works that are therein shall be burned up" (II Peter 3:10). Some erroneously interpret these words to mean that the earth will be utterly destroyed, annihilated, but every student of elementary physics must learn that cumbustion is not a destruction of substance. Combustion, rather, represents a change in state or condition.

The Scriptures make unmistakably clear that the purpose of this cataclysm at the end of the age is not the destruction of the earth, but that the dross may be burned away, that evil and imperfection, the ravages of sin, may be removed. The earth must be cleansed and returned to its original state of perfection not only but more, for the new heavens and the new earth, like redeemed man, shall be elevated to a plane which transcends that of the original creation. In Matthew (19:28) it is called a "regeneration." In Romans (3:21) it is called a "restoration." Again in Romans it is called a "deliverance from the bondage of corruption." Thus Peter is able to write further, "But, according to his promise, we look for new heavens and a new earth, wherein dwelleth righteousness (II Peter 3:13).

Even as our mortal bodies must die in order that they may be fashioned after the glorious body of Christ in the resurrection, so a similar change must transpire in the world we inhabit. The result is to be new heavens and a new earth wherein dwelleth righteousness, and wherein dwelleth the righteous that is, the children of God.

The new heavens and new earth, regenerated, restored, renovated, freed from the bondage of corruption, is to be the seat of the ultimate form of the kingdom of Christ. This is the New Jerusalem. This is the Mount Zion in which are gathered the general assembly and church of the first born, which are written in heaven, the spirits of just men made perfect. This is the heavenly Jerusalem, the city of the living God.

Thus, the trembling of the earth as Christ hanged upon the cross points forward to that great day of the Lord God Almighty when the earth shall tremble in the throes of rebirth and regeneration, so that it may become a redeemed world in which redeemed men may dwell. This is the Christian hope and the Christian faith, that God will redeem us not only but the world in which we live, so that perfected men may dwell together in a perfected world.

We should be presenting a half truth, however, if we were to leave another facet of the story untold. There is another facet to the story, you know. Peter presents it in the passage to which we have already made reference. There one may also read, "But the heavens that now are, and the earth, by the same word have been stored up for fire, being reserved against the day of judgment and destruction of ungodly men" (II Peter 3:7).

These are the alternatives always, life or death, regeneration or destruction, heaven or hell. The quaking of the earth at Calvary speaks of redemption to the children of God, to them who are in Christ. The self-same trembling of the earth at Calvary speaks of eternal condemnation to them who are apart from God and apart from Christ, and therefore, under the wrath of God. What will you have then? Redemption in Christ? A perfect life in a perfect world, reborn in the cleansing fires of God? Or eternal condemnation in the eternal

fires of the wrath of God? The Old Negro spiritual speaks
well when it asks:

> "O my loving brother, when the world's on fire,
> Don't you want God's bosom to be your pillow?
> Hide me over in the rock of ages,
> Rock of ages cleft for me."

11. O Grave, Where Is Thy Victory?

"And the graves were opened; and many bodies of the saints which slept arose." — Matt. 27:52

"And Jesus cried again with a loud voice, and yielded up his Spirit. And, behold, the veil of the temple was rent in two from the top to the bottom; and the earth did quake, and the rocks were rent; and many bodies of the saints who had fallen asleep were raised; and coming forth out of the tombs *after* his resurrection, they entered into the holy city and appeared unto many" (Matt. 27:50-52, ASV).

The opening of the tombs may well be denominated the "fourth miracle of the cross." It was preceded by the unnatural darkness at noonday, the rending of the veil, and the quaking of the earth with the rending of the rocks. Each of these four supernatural events is related to the others in that all of them have a common relationship to the death of Christ. In addition, three of the miracles possess a further inter-relationship. The rending of the veil, the quaking of the earth with the rending of the rocks, and the opening of the graves are all expressly related to the cry of Christ from the cross.

Perhaps this dual inter-relatedness has led to misunderstanding, the misunderstanding of lumping these supernatural events as though they have no independent significance. This is particularly true of the opening of the graves. Many commentators fail to perceive the independent significance, the separateness if you will, of the opening of the graves.

On the one hand, the opening of the graves is commonly regarded as a mere natural consequence of the quaking of the earth. We do not suggest that the earthquake had no bearing upon the opening of the graves. Indeed, the forces which caused the earth to quake undoubtedly opened the graves. We dare not, however, disregard the significance of the fact that only selected graves were opened, that is, the graves of the saints. As a result, we must recognize that God had a specific end in view in the opening of the graves. One might express the distinction in this way. In the earthquake, we see a demonstration of the power of God. In the opening of selected graves, we see his power directed to the accomplishment of a specific goal. The opening of the graves, therefore, may not be regarded as a mere natural consequence of the earthquake. To the contrary, the opening of the graves must be regarded as having a purpose that goes beyond the cause and purpose of the quaking of the earth.

A closely related misconception views the opening of the graves as a mere prelude, an incidental antecedent, to the raising of the bodies. Again, admittedly, a relationship exists between the opening of the graves and the raising of the bodies of the saints. The bodies of the saints which arose came forth from precisely those graves which had been opened by the quaking of the earth. At this point, however, the record must be read with care. The time element must be noted. While the graves were opened by the cry of Christ from the cross on Friday afternoon, the bodies were not raised until after his resurrection on the third day. The tombs were opened on Friday afternoon, but the bodies lay unmoved in the opened graves until after the resurrection of Christ. Then the saints arose.

Why should the graves be opened on Friday afternoon, if the bodies were not to be raised for three days? We propounded this question in a Bible class. One young man gave this answer, "Because there was no earthquake on resurrection morning to open the tombs." Ah, but there was an earthquake on resurrection morning, "a great earthquake," according to Matthew's record. Matthew describes the scene on resurrection morning like this, "And, behold, there was a great earthquake, for the angel of the Lord descended from heaven, and came and rolled away the stone and sat upon it" (Matt. 28:2).

God had the means for opening the tombs on resurrection morning of course. With or without an earthquake, God would have opened the graves on resurrection morning, had this been his purpose. Our faith is not strained by the suggestion that, just as an angel rolled away the stone from before the tomb where the body of Jesus had lain, so God might have sent legions of angels to open legions of graves on resurrection morning. As a matter of record, however, God sent another great earthquake on the morning of the third day. Clearly, God could have used the earthquake on resurrection morning to open the graves of the saints. Men might well have regarded this as an appropriate act, to follow the resurrection of our Lord with an earthquake which would open the graves of the saints.

All this simply serves to emphasize the pertinence of the question, why should God have opened the tombs on Friday afternoon, if the bodies were not to be raised until the morning of the third day? This is the answer: The opening of the graves was in itself a sign. The opening of the graves bears a message from God which is both related to and yet distinct from the fact that the bodies of the saints were raised on the third day. While the two are not unrelated, the opening of the graves has a significance in its own right. If we may propound a hypothetical proposition, had no bodies of the saints been raised on the third day, the opening of the graves at the cry of Christ would not have been without significance. The act of opening the graves, therefore, has independent significance.

The independent significance of the opening of the graves may also be perceived in this: Not only were the bodies untouched by the power of God, but they were also untouched and unattended by men during the entire period prior to their resurrection. How can we be certain? The Jewish Sabbath began at sundown on Friday. This was the reason for haste in dispensing with the body of Christ and the bodies of the two malefactors. By the same token, had anyone touched or attended the bodies lying in their opened graves, the person would have been defiled, and the Sabbath would have been desecrated. Thus the bodies lay in plain view from the time the graves were opened until the morning of the third day when they were raised. This, without question, was intended of God. The graves must lie open, the bodies within them, until the morning of the third day.

Again, all this serves to reiterate the question, What is the peculiar, independent significance of the opening of the graves at the cry of Christ from the cross? The timing or scheduling of events suggests the first answer. The opening of the graves was the Father's stamp of approval on the atoning work of the Son. We have consistently linked the opening of the graves to the cry of Christ from the cross and rightly so. Now we must also note that his cry announced his death. Matthew wrote, "And Jesus cried again with a loud voice, and yielded up his Spirit." The last loud cry from the cross was the "death cry." With this cry, Jesus announced the departure of his soul from his body. Now He would be translated to paradise to await the repentant malefactor who would follow close after.

In the deepest sense his cry, in and of itself, may be said to have had less bearing upon the opening of the graves than did the fact of his death. We shall not go astray if we say the graves were opened by his death, or at a minimum we may say, the graves could not have been opened apart from his death. We must not fail to observe the essential connection between his death and the opening of the graves.

This essential connection may be observed in the death and resurrection of our Lord. When our loved ones are taken in death, we lay great stress upon the resurrection and rightly so. Paul wrote in connection with the bodily resurrection, "If we have hope in Christ in this life only, we are of all men most miserable." But the resurrection is grounded in the fact that the atonement of the cross was acceptable to God. We may say the resurrection was a visible demonstration of God's approval of the atonement of his Son.

Our hope of life is grounded in the death of Christ. He died that we might live. He took our place. He died our death. Therefore, we live, because He died. And the opening of the graves was God's first announcement that He found the

atonement acceptable. We say, "the first announcement," because the great announcement would come on resurrection
morning when the Lord Himself should come forth from the
tomb. But God did not wait until resurrection morning to
declare his pleasure in the atoning death of his Son. In the
very moment the Savior died, in the very moment that He uttered the "death cry," God showed forth his good pleasure
in opening the graves of the saints.

Secondly, the opening of the graves was a witness to the
victory of Christ over the grave. If you have ever thought of
the "victory of Christ over the grave" or of his title, "Victor
over the Grave," as a mere figure of speech, you must do so
no more. When the atonement had been made, when the great
work of redemption had been finished upon the cross, and the
cry burst forth from the lips of Christ, God literally opened
the graves of the saints as a testimony to the victory which had
been won on the cross.

Thus the great cry from the cross was a "victory cry." We
have already noted that the cry from the cross was a "death
cry," but this designation is incomplete and could, perhaps, be
misconstrued, if it were allowed to stand by itself. To many,
indeed to the whole world of unbelief, death signifies defeat.
Nothing could be farther removed from the truth in connection with the death of our Lord. His death was victory,
victory over sin and death and the grave, and therefore, the
death cry was a victory cry.

To grasp this truth, we must remind ourselves that death is
the result of sin. The Scriptures declare, "The wages of sin
is death . . ." (Rom. 6:23), and again, "The soul that sinneth,
it shall die" (Ezek. 18:4). On the cross the price of sin was
paid. When the justice of God had been satisfied, the death
penalty was removed. Again, once death is removed, the grave
is denied its victim. Therefore, when the price of sin was paid,
and death was done away, He gave the victory cry, and the
graves of the saints were opened. This is why Paul could burst
forth with the joyous exclamation, "O death, where is thy
sting? O grave, where is thy victory? . . . Thanks be to God

who giveth us the victory through our Lord Jesus Christ" (I Cor. 15:55-57).

Are you impressed by the fact that the grave is a constant, silent witness to the price which God has fixed on sin? And not for us alone or for men who are limited to a particular area. The world over, the grave is a testimony, not only to the sin of man but to the price God has fixed upon it.

Admittedly, the graves which were opened at the cry of Christ appear to have been limited to the area in close proximity to the cross. This we deduce from the fact that after his resurrection on the third day, when the bodies of the saints were raised, Matthew reports, they "went into the holy city and appeared unto many." Thus the victory appears to have been announced within a relatively limited area. The reason is clear enough. No one outside the area, no one who was unaware of the death of the cross, would have understood the witness of the opened graves.

But the graves themselves are everywhere, the world around. As we bring our Christian witness to bear, as the gospel is preached to men of every tongue and tribe and nation, it is part of our task to reveal to men the meaning of death and the grave. The graves all over the world are a testimony to the curse sin has brought upon the human race. Nor may we allow ourselves to forget. When you pass the burial ground and look out over the earth with its mounds of brown and green, do you say to yourself, "This is what sin has done to man"? Do you say to yourself, "Therein lies the evidence that God will not permit sin to go unpunished"?

To us who continue to hold the old faith, once for all delivered to the saints, the unbeliever and the theological liberal say, "Your religion is so grim. God isn't like that. God is love. God does not demand of men that they shall pay the price of sin." If this were true, why then did Jesus die upon the cross? If God does not punish sin, why then was the Son of God crucified? Our forefathers in the faith declared. "Rather than that sin should go unpunished, God punished sin in the Person of his own beloved Son." True, and the grave continues to testify to all men that the curse upon sin is death.

A clergyman who should not be dignified with the title, "Minister of the Gospel," once addressed a ministerial meeting in Chicago. His thesis was that the Biblical ideas of sin and salvation are archaic. He said, "The idea of a God of justice who will demand satisfaction for human sin is primitive and unworthy of twentieth century man." When he had finished, a member of the audience asked, "Have you ever conducted a funeral?" He replied, "Of course, many of them." To which the questioner rejoined, "That is God's answer to sin." Indeed! All over the world are the graves, everyone of them a witness and a testimony to the curse of God upon sin.

Perhaps you have heard men who sought to explain away the virgin birth of our Lord. Perhaps you have heard them as they sought to explain away the atoning character of his death. Perhaps you have heard them deny his resurrection, his ascension, and his bodily return at the end of the age. Now, consider, have you found anyone who could explain death away? All over the world, the grave stands as a witness to all men that the curse of sin is real and terrible.

The price of sin must be paid! Jesus paid the price when He bore in his own body our sin. When the price of sin had been paid to the last drop of his precious blood, then He gave the victory cry, and God opened the graves! Then Paul could exclaim, "O death, where is thy sting? O grave, where is thy victory?" For death was swallowed up in victory upon the cross. When the price of sin was paid, the death penalty was removed. Then God opened the graves to announce to men that the curse had been lifted.

Thirdly, the opening of the graves with the inter-related miracles, was a demonstration of his victory over the principalities and powers of darkness. The victory of Christ, as it is set forth in Scripture, was a multiple victory. Sin, death, the grave, hell — and Satan no less — are always linked together when Scripture speaks of his victory.

In writing to the Church at Colosse, Paul declares that Christ blotted out "the handwriting of ordinances that was against us . . . and took it out of the way, nailing it to the cross" (Col. 2:14). Then Paul continues in the next verse to make this significant declaration, "And having spoiled principalities and powers, He made a show of them openly, triumphing over them" (Col. 2:15) . In triumphing over the principalities and powers, our Lord made a show of them openly. One may rightly hold that this has a deeper significance than the opening of the graves, but surely no one will dispute that his triumph was nowhere more clear. Never did He more openly display his victory over the very powers of darkness.

Paul's declaration concerning the triumph of Christ over the principalities and powers of darkness should be immediately related to Jesus' instructive statement on the strong man's house. He asked, " . . . how can one enter into a strong man's house, and spoil his goods, except he first bind the strong man? And then he will spoil his house" (Matt. 12:29) . So the cry from the cross invaded Satan's domain. Though he is called "the prince of this world" (John 12:31) , he was brought to his knees by the victory cry from the cross. Thus Jesus displayed his power, opening the very graves of the dead.

The grave cannot withstand the power of God. The earth cannot hold its dead. The sea cannot retain its captives. No power on earth nor in hell can hold the bodies of those for whom Christ died. The power of the grave was broken once and forever on the cross. This is the testimony of the opened graves. Even as He gave the victory cry, and the graves were opened, so in that last day at the sound of the trump of God the graves shall be opened.

Fourthly, the opening of the graves is a testimony to the limited or particular nature of the atonement. Consider the record. Not all graves were opened. Nor three days later, when the dead came forth, did all arise. These, we are told, were the "saints." The graves which were opened were those of the children of God. The all-seeing eye of God searched out the earth, penetrating dirt and rock, selecting the graves of the faithful. These, and these only, were wrenched apart and cast open.

In the Scriptural illiteracy of our age men neither understand nor care to understand that Christ died not for men in the mass but for those who were given Him of the Father.

They sense neither the beauty nor the tenderness of his declaration, "I am the Good Shepherd, and know my sheep and am known of mine . . . and I lay down my life for the sheep" (John 10:14-15). Not for the goats, you understand, but for the sheep! Here was the demonstration of this truth, even as He hanged upon the cross. When He gave the victory cry, the graves were opened, but not all graves, only those of the sheep of his pasture. We should hear again the words of John, "He calleth his own sheep by name and leadeth them out" (John 10:3). Yes, we understand, this applies to the calling unto salvation, but who would dispute that He called his own sheep by name, even as He opened their graves by his mighty cry from the cross?

Moreover, this is what we may expect on that great resurrection morning to come when the dead in Christ shall rise and share the glory of his resurrection. At his coming, land and sea shall bring forth their dead, but again, not merely as a mass of men but as those for whom Christ died. The voice of the archangel shall call out the name of Paul, and Paul shall rise. The voice of the archangel shall call out the name of Peter, and Peter shall rise. More important to me, selfish as it may appear, is that the voice of the archangel shall call out my name, and I too shall rise. Then, too, shall He say to the Father, "I have kept them . . . that Thou gavest Me, and not one of them has perished . . ." (John 17:12). This is why we may sing with an assurance born of faith:

> When the trumpet of the Lord shall sound,
> And time shall be no more,
> When the morning breaks eternal bright and fair,
> When the saved of earth shall gather
> Over on the other shore,
> And the roll is called up yonder,
> I'll be there.

If the faith which is in Christ Jesus is in your heart, you too may sing with assurance, "I'll be there." Your name is written into the Lamb's Book of Life. He lay down his life for the sheep. More, He calleth his own sheep by name, both now and in the last day. Then we shall rise, whole men in body and soul.

Fifthly, the opening of the graves is a witness to the exclusive, unique, once-for-all nature of the salvation which was wrought by Christ. We state merely the obvious when we point out that the graves which were opened by the cry from the cross were clearly the graves of those who had been taken in death *before* Christ had wrought the sacrifice of the cross. How long before? This is irrelevant. How long had these bodies lain in their graves? This is irrelevant. One fact is clear: All these had died before the sacrifice of the cross was made.

Thus God opened the graves of the Old Testament saints to demonstrate their dependence upon Christ for the hope of life beyond the grave. Their hope, like ours, is grounded in his death and resurrection. Hence the opening of the graves provided a dramatic demonstration of an ageless principle, namely, "By grace are ye saved through faith; and that not of yourselves: it is the gift of God: Not of works, lest any man should boast" (Eph. 2:8-9). We must be vitally aware that God's Old Testament people, the church of the Old Testament, stand in the same relationship to Christ as does the church of the New Testament.

This is one aspect of the confession we make in terms of the Apostle's Creed, "I believe in . . . a holy catholic [universal] Church." We do not speak merely of a worldwide church in a particular generation, but of *the church* which is a cross-section of all generations from the beginning to the end of time.

Is this a Biblical concept? Of course! With specific reference to the Old Testament period, we read in the eleventh chapter of Hebrews, "By faith Abel . . . . By faith Enoch . . . . By faith Abraham . . . .By faith Moses," and so on through the abbreviated "roll-call" of the Old Testament saints. Nor can we have any doubt concerning the nature of their faith. Of Abraham, Paul wrote, the gospel was preached to him beforehand (Gal. 3:8). Was this necessary? Indeed, for Paul wrote in the same chapter, " . . . no man is justified by the keeping of the law in the sight of God" (Gal. 3:11). And, therefore, Paul also wrote, " . . . Abraham believed, and it was accounted unto him for righteousness" (Gal. 3:6). Abraham was confronted with the same gospel as twentieth century man, and he was saved in the same way, that is, by grace through faith.

Can we be certain that Christ was the objective of their faith? If anyone has doubt, the answer is spelled out concerning Moses in the epistle to the Hebrews. Of Moses, we read, "By faith Moses . . . refused to be called the son of Pharoah's daughter; choosing rather to suffer affliction with the people of God, than to enjoy the pleasures of sin for a season; Esteeming the reproach of *Christ* greater riches than the treasures in Egypt . . ." (Heb. 11:24-26).

In a generation when men have "itching ears" and "will not endure sound doctrine," we must continually reiterate the only principle of salvation set forth in the Word of God, to wit, by grace through faith. Incredible though it be, some would tell us that men were saved by the keeping of the law in the Old Testament era. They call themselves "fundamentalists," but they are nothing of the sort. They degrade Christ and dishonor his death by proposing a means of salvation other than the death of the cross. Whether in the Old Testament era or the New, "Neither is there salvation in any other: for there is none other name under heaven given among men, whereby we must be saved" (Acts 4:12). Therefore, God opened the graves of the Old Testament saints to demonstrate their dependence upon Christ for salvation and life.

What a testimony this should continue to be to the world of unregenerate men, for men continue to believe in salvation by works, rather than by grace through faith. I say to the man on the street, "Will you not fear to face God in that last day?" He replies, "I have nothing to fear. I live as best I know how. I provide for my family. I do harm to no man. That is enough for me." "But you do not come to the church to worship God. You do not acknowledge Christ as your Savior and Lord. You neither live nor speak as though you have a responsibility to God."

He answers, "We are all the children of God. If I live decently and honestly, all will be well with my soul." How wrong he is! How many bodies of decent, honest men lay in graves that were not opened by the cry of Christ from the cross. How many bodies of respectable men, "good" men, lay in graves that were undisturbed by the cry that shook the earth.

Ah, no. There is only one who can take sin away, and He is the Christ. There is only one who can take away the penalty of sin. There is only one who can take away the curse of sin. There is only one who can take death away. There is only one who can take the grave away. That one is the Christ of the cross, who bore in his own body our sin, who took upon Himself the penalty of our sin, who took upon Himself the curse that was due to us, who died that we might live, who rose that we might rise, and who is seated at the right hand of power, awaiting that day when He shall come upon the clouds of heaven in power and great glory, and all the angels with Him. When the trumpet of the Lord shall sound, and time shall be no more, then shall the archangel call the roll of those whose names are written into the Lamb's Book of Life.

Is it any wonder that the saints rejoice to sing:

> I will praise my dear Redeemer;
> His triumphant power I'll tell;
> How the victory He giveth
> Over sin and death and Hell.
>
> Sing, O sing of my Redeemer,
> With His blood He purchased me,
> On the cross He sealed my pardon,
> Paid the debt and made me free.

12. After His Resurrection, Bodies Raised

"And the graves were opened; and many bodies of the saints which slept arose." — Matt. 27:52

Matthew writes, "And many bodies of the saints which had fallen asleep were raised." Thus he describes the fifth in a series of miracles all of which center about the cross and the death of Christ. After recording the darkness which fell at noon, the first of the "miracles of the cross," Matthew depicts a series of supernatural events within the compass of a few sentences. The lingual picture is presented in these words, "And Jesus cried again with a loud voice, and yielded up his Spirit. And behold, the veil of the temple was rent in twain from the top to the bottom; and the earth did quake, and the rocks were rent; and the tombs were opened; and many bodies of the saints that had fallen asleep were raised; and coming forth out of the tombs after his [Christ's] resurrection they entered into the holy city and appeared unto many."

The raising of the bodies of the saints has been dubbed the "misplaced miracle"; not misplaced in the plan of God, you understand, but misplaced in the minds of those who treat the Scriptural record carelessly. One frequently encounters the assumption that the bodies of the saints were raised when the graves were opened. This would place the resurrection of the saints, if such it may be termed, at the time of our Lord's death. Actually, the record places the raising of the bodies of the saints subsequent to the resurrection of our Lord. Nonetheless, this the "fifth miracle of the cross," is related to the other miracles in that it is one in a chain of inter-related events. The raising of the bodies followed from and was dependent upon the opening of the graves, even though, time-wise, they were separatd by a considerable interval. The opening of the graves, in turn, was accomplished by the quak-ing of the earth. The rending of the veil precedes all these. And each of these events followed upon the cry of Christ from the cross.

This miracle stands apart from the others in that, while all have supernatural aspects, this one, like the rending of the veil, cannot conceivably be traced to so-called "natural causes." In the instance of the darkness which fell upon the earth as Christ hanged upon the cross, the latest astronomical studies have failed to discover any conceivable natural causes. To the contrary, our present knowledge of celestial mechanics rules out the possibility of any known cause. Still, the most astute scientists must confess that they know so little of the intricate workings of this vast universe created by God that no one can presume to determine what means God may have employed in the vast outreaches of space in order to bring the strange, unnatural, noonday darkness to pass.

In the case of the earthquake, historians, scientists, and phys-ical geologists alike must confess that none other like it has been reported in all recorded history; yet, no man professes such expert knowledge of the inner mechanics of the earth as to be able to say what forces God may have used in bringing that most unusual, unexplained earthquake to pass.

When one comes to the raising of the bodies of the saints, however, he is confronted by a matter which clearly involves pure supernaturalism. No forces or means are known to man, even in the latter half of the twentieth century, whereby life can be created. Medical scientists confess that, while they can outline the steps which eventuate in birth, they cannot begin to explain the "how" of the birth of a child.

So when life is gone, there is no power, knowledge, or force known to man whereby life can be re-created or restored. It is instructive to note, while medical science has taken long strides in the prevention and healing of disease, on the basic issues of life and death, medical science is helpless. No doctor, medical scientist, bio-chemist or pathologist, even to this day, has been able to produce a means for the raising of the dead or the reintroduction of life. Thus, when we learn the dead were raised in connection with the death of Christ, we must recognize, this was a case of pure supernaturalism. It was the immediate working of God, nothing less.

To remove any possibility of misunderstanding, perhaps we should spend a moment with this consideration. When we say, this was the "immediate" work of God, we mean that God used no known instrumentalities or forces to accomplish his purposes. We confess that God governs and controls all things. It is part and parcel of our faith that all things are brought to pass by the activity of God. Usually the activity of God follows a well defined pattern, precisely because He is a God of order. When man is able to recognize and define a particular pattern of divine activity, he refers to this pattern as a "natural law." Sometimes, however, God interrupts the usual pattern or order of his activity. The unusual phenomenon which results is then termed a "miracle." But miracles may be produced either by the unusual employment of "natural" causes or by the direct action of God, that is, without the use of intermediate forces. The raising of the bodies of the saints represents the latter situation. It was an act of the will and word of God. The saints were raised without the use of any intermediate instrumentality.

Consider, further, when the skeptics encounter a situation such as this, what can they say? They can offer no possible human or natural explanation. This is what they seek to do in many instances, you know. They seek to offer a natural explanation for a miraculous event, as if the possibility of an explanation ruled out the handiwork of God. For us who believe, this is not the case. We know that God employs "natural" forces to accomplish his own purposes daily. By faith, we see his hand behind all "natural" forces. In the raising of the dead, however, the scoffer is confronted with a different situation, one which permits of no natural explanation. What, then, shall the scoffers do with a situation such as this? They have but one answer. "It simply did not happen," they say.

Because this is the case, God who plans all things from the beginning, leaves no stone unturned in a situation such as this. God so arranged the circumstances that no conceivable doubt might exist as to what happened here. As marvelous as the event itself is the way in which God arranged the smallest detail. He, who takes knowledge of the sparrow as it falls from the tree, prepared the minutest details and particulars of this amazing event, the raising of the dead.

One might ask, "Were these men really dead and buried?" To this, their friends and loved ones, those who had attended them in death and burial, could readily testify. True, some may well have passed on before the contemporary generation had been born; for them, there would be no family, no loved ones to testify. But note this, the tombs lay open from Good Friday afternoon until resurrection morning. This means that the dead bodies, that is, such remains as there were, lay in plain view for all to see. Realistically, it could not have been a pretty picture. One may well suspect that the people would have acted quickly to remove the offensive sight, to close the graves, to repair the tombs, to dispose of the bodies — if it had not been for one fact, the intervening day was the Sabbath.

When Jesus cried from the cross, the sacrifices were about to begin in the temple. Sundown, the beginning of the Sabbath, was at hand. There was no time to close the graves or repair the tombs. For anyone to have touched these graves or the bodies that lay within them would have been to desecrate the Sabbath not only, but the person would have been rendered ceremonially unclean. They were compelled to leave the graves lying open! They were compelled to leave the dead bodies in plain view! This was precisely the purpose of God. These bodies must lie exposed. They must be viewed by all who passed by as they lay in their opened graves. All who viewed them were to become witnesses that the dead had truly been raised.

No, it was not a pleasant sight, but it was a necessary one, necessary as a testimony to all ages and generations to come that those who were raised on resurrection morning had been dead and buried in all reality. In addition, when God had brought them forth from their graves, He sent them into the city of Jersualem where, we read, " ... they were seen of many." Those who had passed by the opened graves and the broken tombs on the Sabbath day, those who had viewed the dead lying in their opened graves, were now confronted by the dead who had been raised. They were compelled to testify that God had indeed raised the dead and sent them forth from their graves.

Notice Matthew's statement a second time. "Coming forth out of the tombs after his resurrection," writes Matthew, "they entered into the holy city and appeared unto many." And that is all! There is nothing further in the record. The sparseness of the record should cause one to observe that Matthew's statement is remarkable, not only for what it says, but for what it does not say.

Consider the record as though it were a newspaper account. Note the apparent omissions in Matthew's statement. Who were the saints who were raised? No identifications are made. Did their number include some of the prophets of the Old Testament, men who could have spoken to the people of the fulfillment of their own writings in the person and work of Christ? Could their number have included John the Baptist, who had been slain but a little earlier for his testimony concerning Christ? Again, how many of the saints were raised? What did they do in Jerusalem? Did they preach to the people? Did those who had died more recently, and whose families remained intact, return to their families and lead "normal" lives? What became of the others?

These may be questions which are dictated by mere curiosity, but there are still other questions, vital questions, significant questions, that might have been put to these men. They had just returned from the abode of the blessed dead. They had been assembled with the white robed multitude who surround the throne of God. Consider the things they might have related, had God permitted them to disclose the nature of that other world which opens at the far end of the valley of the shadow. And what did God permit them to tell? Even this we do not know. We know that Paul was permitted to see heavenly things in a vision which he was not permitted to recount. So these men may have been forbidden of God to speak of the things they had seen and experienced in the other world.

Had I been present in those days, and had I been permitted to see these men and speak with them, how many are the questions I might have asked. I would have asked, "What is the nature of that blessed land? What did you do when you were there?" And more personally, I would have asked about those whom I had known and loved, and who have gone on. You would undoubtedly want to do likewise. All or most of us have lost some whom we were permitted to love for a time. If one should come back from the land of the blessed dead today, would you not want to ask about Mother, about Dad, about sons or daughters, about little ones who have been taken away? So, you see, the record of Matthew leaves matters untouched which appear very vital to us.

There are still other questions. What became of those who were raised from the dead? Were they soon removed again from the land of the living? Did they pass through death again? Or were they lifted bodily out of the world after the manner of Enoch who walked with God, and he was not, for God took him? Or again, after the manner of Elijah who was transported out of the world in a flaming chariot?

If you were to ask, "Why have we no record of these things? Why are we given so little information on these matters in which we are so vitally interested, the issues of life and death, the matter of life beyond the grave?" I would answer, "For the best of reasons. Additional information might well have diffused our attention, obscuring the one all-important issue, that these men arose and were seen by many, who could testify that once they were dead, but now they were alive. If we can be certain of this one thing, the power of God to raise the dead, then we can be certain that God will take care of all the rest, which is merely a matter of detail." These, therefore, are the facts. (1) They were dead. (2) They were buried. (3)

They were raised from the dead. (4) They entered the city. (5) They were seen of many.

Having established the one essential fact, that the dead were raised, we must examine the nature of the resurrection which took place. The fact of significance for our attention is that the graves were opened prior to the raising of the bodies. Someone may say, "Of course. How else? Is it not only natural that the graves must be opened before the bodies could be raised?"

To answer this question one must turn to the resurrection of Christ. Concerning our Lord's resurrection, Matthew records, an angel descended from heaven and came and rolled away the stone. Those who had come to the grave early on resurrection morning looked into the tomb from whence the stone had been rolled aside. But Christ was not there. Nor did Christ come forth when the stone was rolled away. By no means. He was long since gone! You see the glorified, resurrection body is not limited either by time or space. The stone was not rolled away from the tomb in which Christ had been laid so that He might come forth. He had already arisen. The stone was rolled away so that his disciples might look in. And in that great resurrection morning to come there will be no need to open tombs or graves, for the glorified body is neither limited nor contained by any material substance.

If this be true, however, why were the graves of the saints opened so that they might be raised and come forth? This points to the heart of the matter: They were not raised with glorified bodies. To employ the language of Paul, the "natural body" was not, in this instance, raised a "spiritual body" (I Cor. 15:44). The resurrection of the saints was similar, for example, to the resurrection of Lazarus, the brother of Mary and Martha. You will recall that Lazarus had died and was laid in the tomb. When Jesus spoke of bringing him back from the dead, the sisters replied, "But Lord, the odors of decay are already present." Little did they realize that decay and decomposition are no problem to God. Jesus went to the tomb. Then the matter we must note came to pass. Jesus commanded, "Roll ye away the stone." Only after the stone had been rolled away did Jesus call Lazarus forth. So it was with the saints who were raised. The graves must be opened in order that they might come forth.

In these cases, we must conclude, a recomposition or a reconstitution of the original, natural body was effected. They were raised with the same body which had been laid in the grave. How can we be certain that this was the case? Hear these words from the pen of Paul, "But now hath Christ been raised from the dead, the first fruits of them that sleep. . . . so also shall all in Christ be made alive. But each in his own order: Christ, the first fruits; then they that are Christ's at his coming. Then cometh the end when He shall deliver up the kingdom to God, even the Father" (I Cor. 15:20-24). This statement places the time of the resurrection, that is, the time of the resurrection unto glory, when the children of God shall receive glorified bodies, at the end of time.

From it, we infer, that all prior instances of the dead being raised, such as are recorded in the Old Testament and in the New Testament, were a return to the life of this world in the natural body. This is the reason that some Biblical scholars refer to these instances as "revivals" rather than as "resurrections." It was a "revival" of the old body, rather than a "resurrection" of the new body. Perhaps the use of these two terms represents a mere babbling in semantics, but certainly a distinction must be made between the resurrection unto glory and the return of various individuals to the life of this world prior to the end of time.

The son of the widow at Sarepta (I Kings 17:17-24), the Shunammite's son (II Kings 4:8-37), and he who was raised when his physical remains came into contact with the bones of Elisha (II Kings 13:20-21), were all instances of "revival," if one may use that term in contradistinction to "resurrection." So it was also with the son of the widow of Nain (Luke 7:11-17), the daughter of Jairus (Matt. 9:18-26), and Lazarus (John 11:1-45), all of whom were raised by Jesus during his ministry. They were "revived," rather than "resurrected." Such was the coming forth of the bodies of the saints which followed the death and resurrection of Christ. Herein lay the necessity for opening the graves. The natural bodies could not come forth, unless the graves were opened.

None of this should be taken to imply, however, that the raising of the bodies of the saints was anything less than a miracle. The raising of the dead under any circumstances lies within the province of God alone. And God had a great purpose in the raising of the bodies of the saints. It was, in truth, a foreshadowing of that which is to come. As such, we may learn its significance for us. What does it mean to us?

First, the raising of the bodies of the saints was a demonstration of the power of God to restore the body. In the great resurrection morning to come we shall rise with glorified bodies to be certain, bodies like unto the glorious resurrection body of Christ, but that body is based upon, grounded in, and essentially related to the body which we now inhabit. Paul compares the relationship between our present bodies and those we shall receive in the resurrection to the relationship between a kernel of wheat which is planted in the ground, and the plant which springs forth from it in due season (I Cor. 15:35-38) .

This fact, apparently, is a source of difficulty for some. They raise various objections. They think of those who were maimed and wounded in war, those who have lost limbs, and those whose bodies were broken. All such objections stem from one fact, the inability of man to fully comprehend that God is as omnipotent as man is helpless. Here, in the raising of the bodies of the saints, is God's declaration that He, with the infinite, almighty power which belongs to God alone, can restore the broken, bleeding, decayed, decalcified bodies of a broken humanity with a word from his sovereign lips.

Secondly, the raising of the bodies of the saints was a demonstration of the power of God to reunite bodies and souls which are separated in the time of physical death. The preacher in Ecclesiastes pointed to the essential nature of physical death when he wrote, "Then shall the dust return to the earth as it was, and the spirit shall return to God who gave it" (Eccles. 12:7) .

This is the exact situation which existed with reference to the bodies of the saints before they were raised. At some time in the past, for some a shorter time, for some a longer time, each of them had experienced death, physical death. The souls of the saints had been translated into blessedness in the presence of God. Their bodies had been laid in the graves and tombs. In the graves their bodies had passed through the process of decay and dissolution. "From the dust thou wast taken, and to the dust thou shalt return" said God, and to the dust they had returned. Of some, those who had died in ages past, there was nought remaining but dust intermingled with the dust of the earth in which they were laid.

Then in a moment of time, in the twinkling of an eye, God, who had created the human body from the dust of the earth in the beginning, now re-created these bodies, returned to them the souls which once they had housed, and sent them forth from the graves.

Thirdly, the raising of the bodies of the saints points to the great resurrection morning when all the dead of all ages shall rise. In the committal service for the body we read, "Forasmuch as it hath pleased Almighty God to take out of this world the soul of our departed brother, we therefore commit his body to the ground, earth to earth, ashes to ashes, dust to dust; looking for the general resurrection in the last day, and the life of the world to come through our Lord Jesus Christ; at whose second coming in glorious majesty to judge the world, the earth and sea shall give up their dead; and the corruptible bodies of those who sleep in Him shall be changed, and made like unto his glorious body; according to the working whereby He is able to subdue all things unto Himself."

Perhaps we should interject a note on the general nature of the resurrection lest any misunderstand. Nothing we have said should be taken to imply that the dead shall not all be raised together. The book of Daniel spells it out like this, "And many of them that sleep in the dust of the earth shall awake, some to everlasting life, and some to shame and everlasting contempt" (Dan. 12:2). Nor can there be any doubt concerning the "when" of it. Jesus said, "Marvel not at this:

for the hour is coming, in the which all that are in the graves shall hear his voice, And *shall come forth;* they that have done good, unto the resurrection of life; and they that have done evil, unto the resurrection of damnation" (John 5:28-29) .

There is but one resurrection, a general resurrection of all the dead. Why, then, have we concerned ourselves only with the resurrection of the saints? Because this is our hope. By faith we fully anticipate that we shall rise, not unto condemnation but unto glory. Looking forward to the general resurrection in the last day! And what a resurrection it will be for the children of God! "... sown in corruption ... raised in incorruption; sown in dishonor ... raised in glory; sown in weakness ... raised in power; sown a natural body ... raised a spiritual body" (I Cor. 15:42-44) .

Then we shall gather on the shores of the crystal sea, at the foot of Mount Zion, the General Assembly and Church of the First Born, whose names are written in heaven, the spirits of just men made perfect. Then we shall join the angelic host as they sing the anthems of heaven, "Worthy is the Lamb that hath been slain to receive the power, and riches, and wisdom, and might, and honor, and glory, and blessing. . . . Unto him that sitteth on the throne, and unto the Lamb, be the blessing, and the honor, and the glory, and the dominion, forever and ever" (Rev. 5:12-13) .